Perth Bush, City Walks

By
Paul Amyes

Woodslane Press Pty Ltd
Unit 7/5 Vuko Place
Warriewood, NSW 2102
Australia
Email: info@woodslane.com.au
Tel: (02) 9970 5111 Fax: (02) 9970 5002 www.travelandoutdoor.bookcentre.com.au

First published in Australia in 2010 by Woodslane Press, reprinted 2010, 2011

Copyright © 2010 Woodslane Press Pty Ltd; text and photographs © 2010 Paul Amyes

All rights reserved. Apart from any fair dealing for the purposes of study, research or review, as permitted under Australian copyright law, no part of this publication may be reproduced, distributed, or transmitted in any other form or by any means, including photocopying, recording, or other electronic or mechanical methods, without the prior written permission of the publisher. For permission requests, write to the publisher, addressed "Attention: Permissions Coordinator", at the address above. Every effort has been made to obtain permissions relating to information reproduced in this publication. The information in this publication is based upon the current state of commercial and industry practice and the general circumstances as at the date of publication. No person shall rely on any of the contents of this publication and the publisher and the author expressly exclude all liability for direct and indirect loss suffered by any person resulting in any way from the use or reliance on this publication or any part of it. Any opinions and advice are offered solely in pursuance of the author's and publisher's intention to provide information, and have not been specifically sought.

National Library of Australia Cataloguing-in-Publication entry

Author:	Amyes, Paul, 1963-
Title:	Perth's best bush, coast & city walks : the full colour guide to over 40 fantastic walks / Paul Amyes.
Edition:	1st ed.
ISBN:	9781921606793 (pbk.)
Notes:	Includes index.
Subjects:	Hiking--Western Australia--Perth Region--Guidebooks. Walking--Western Australia--Perth Region--Guidebooks.. Perth (W.A.)--Guidebooks.
Dewey Number:	796.51099411

Printed in China by
Designed by Coral Lee
Main cover image: Penguin Island in Shoalwater Islands Marine Park off the coast of Rockingham (walk 29)

Contents

Regional map iii
Introduction 1
    Walk grades and times 2
    Walking with children 2
    Be prepared 2
    Care for the environment 4
    Track closures 5
Walks at a glance 6

Perth's Best Bush, Coast & City Walks
    Metropolitan walks 11
    Swan and Canning Rivers 31
    Wetlands 77
    Coastal Walks 101
    The Darling Range 135

Location maps
    South of Perth 189
    Central Perth 190-191
    East of Perth 192-193
Index 194
Transperth map 197
CAT routes map 198-199
About the author 200
Acknowledgements 200
Other books from Woodslane 202
Feedback 204

Introduction

Perth, with its great year-round climate, is justifiably famous for its outdoor lifestyle, to which walking is perfectly suited. The variety of locations within the Perth Metropolitan Area means that there are walks to suit people of all ages, abilities and interests - throughout the year. Within the city are national parks that are home to some of Western Australia's unique flora and fauna; the Swan River is the jewel in Perth's crown and provides access to an ever-changing natural environment; and the coastal areas provide Perth with a vital form of summer relief and some of the world's best beaches. In all, this book contains forty two walks that cover over 240 kilometres of Perth's best walking trails.

Public transport

Each walk indicates how best to travel to the start of the walk, and how to return to the start (if necessary) once you've finished, but you should always confirm service availability or times with any public transport provider before setting out. For information on most services, either T 13 62 13 or visit www.transperth.wa.gov.au.

Introduction

Walk grades and times

Every walk includes the grade, estimated time and distance. Of course, estimating grades and times can be a little tricky. In this book they generally err on the side of caution, but you will soon figure out whether your own pace is faster or slower than what's indicated.

Easy: Suitable for all ages, but take care with children.

Medium: Some tricky rocks or steps, or requiring good fitness or navigational skills.

Hard: Experienced walkers only.

Do not underestimate how much the total ascent or descent influences how hard you'll find a walk: a 6 kilometre walk that's relatively level will take half the time of a 6 kilometre walk that descends and then ascends 600 metres.

Walking with children

Many of the walks are suitable for children, although only a parent can judge whether the distance and grade is manageable for their child. Smaller children may be carried in a backpack and a few of the walks are paved and suitable for a stroller. The key to walking safely with children is supervision. With one child and two adults, almost any walk in this book is

possible, and arguably quite safe. With thirty children and one adult, however, there would be risks in even the easiest walk in this book. Probably the best advice is to start with the easy walks and see how you (and your children) fare. If you decide to try one of the harder grades, make sure you have lots of time and at least one adult per child.

Be prepared

Always carry drinking water. It is not wise to depend upon finding water when bush walking in Western Australia: in summer it can be nonexistent and in winter water runoff carries the risk of contamination. In summer,

Introduction

you will need at least two litres per person for every two hours of walking (a frozen plastic bottle will ensure cold water for hours), hydration packs such as those made by CamelBack make this easy to carry. In winter, you can probably make do with a bit less. Also take some food with you. Hunger is a major cause of fatigue and if you're inexperienced (or walking with others who are inexperienced) food offers a chance to catch your breath and re-energize.

Know your route and, in the bush, don't walk alone. Apart from the shortest of walks, you are best to walk with a companion, and on long walks, three people are better than two. Always make sure there's someone who knows where you are going and when to expect you back. Remember that on some walks in this book, particularly those in the Darling Range forests, you will not be able to get a mobile phone signal. Taking a regional map could be a good idea.

Wear a hat and sunscreen. Regardless of the time of year, take sunscreen with you and wear a hat (www.cancerwa.asn.au/prevention/sunsmart/how-to-be-sunsmart). Be aware of the risk of heatstroke and if possible try to walk early or late in the day. If you cannot avoid walking in the middle of a hot day, avoid exposed ridges, cliff tops and fire trails.

Good footwear is essential - there is nothing more miserable than poor quality shoes rubbing and causing blisters while walking. Choose your shoes carefully - no thongs or heels - and do not plan to break in a new pair of shoes just before heading off on a full day's walk. Fully enclosed shoes, although hot in summer will provide support and protection for your feet. Training shoes may be suitable on paved paths but in the bush,

Introduction

where the surface maybe more irregular, loose walking shoes or light weight hiking boots will be more suitable. Stay clear of long grass or thick vegetation.

Be respectful

Some of the walks in this book will take you to or very close to Aboriginal sacred sites. Please respect these special places as you would say a church or a temple.

Care for the environment

Please respect the environment when you go out walking by following these basic rules:

- Do not disturb any native animals and do not pick wildflowers.
- Many of the walks described within this book allow you to take dogs. Please take them on a lead and clean up after them. For those areas such as national parks and water catchment areas where dogs are prohibited please do not take your dog.
- Place all litter in bins where provided, if there are no bins carry your litter home with you.
- Stay on the paths provided, this prevents erosion and enables you to be found if you get lost.

Introduction

- If there are no toilets, bury human waste at least 15 cm deep and at least 100 metres away from any water source.
- Be responsible about fire. At certain times of year it only takes a single spark to create a fire that can get out of control and destroy thousands of hectares within a matter of hours, often threatening lives and property. For this reason, total fire bans are imposed on days of extreme fire danger.
- It's good practice to keep your walking, or camping gear clean between different environments, particularly in areas affected by 'dieback', a soil-borne pathogen called Phytophthora cinnamomi that invades the roots of plants, starving them of water and nutrients. Dieback is spread when soil or roots are moved, possibly via your boots, car or tent. Dieback areas are usually closed to the public but boot cleaning stations are provided for high-risk walking tracks.

Track closures

Tracks are sometimes temporarily closed for maintenance, or other reasons such as storm damage, local flooding. bushfires or unsafe footpaths. For information regarding National Park track closures, phone the Department of Environment and Conservation on (08) 9295 2244 or visit www.dec.wa.gov.au/content/category/33/910/1558. For areas outside National Parks, contact the relevant local council.

Walks at a glance

Walks at a glance

Walk	Page	Distance (km)	Time	Grade
Metropolitan Walks				
1 Perth City Walk	12	6.7 circuit	2 hrs	Easy
2 King's Park Explorer	18	7 circuit	1 hr 30 mins	Easy
3 Fremantle Culture Vulture Walk	22	4.2 circuit	1 hr	Easy
4 Guildford Heritage Trail	26	3.8 circuit	1 hr	Easy
Swan and Canning River				
5 John George Walk Trail	32	4 one way	1 hr 15 mins	Easy
6 Claisebrook Cove	36	2.3 circuit	45 mins	Easy
7 A Tale of Two Bridges	40	10 circuit	2 hrs 30 mins	Easy
8 Pelican Point - Matilda Bay	44	4 circuit	1 hr 15 mins	Easy
9 Point Walter and Blackwall Reach	48	4.3 circuit	1 hr	Medium
10 Claremont Foreshore	52	5 one way	1 hr 30 mins	Medium
11 Freshwater Bay	56	2.3 circuit	45 mins	Easy
12 Rocky Bay - Garanup Park	60	5.7 return	1 hr 45 mins	Medium
13 From the River to the Sea	64	6.5 one way	2 hrs	Easy
14 Deep Water Point	68	8 circuit	2 hrs	Easy
15 Woodloes Walk	72	4 circuit	1 hour	Easy
The Wetlands				
16 Yanchep Wetlands Walk Trail	78	2.6 circuit	45 mins	Easy
17 Yanchep Caves Walk Trail	81	4.5 circuit	1 hr 30 mins	Easy
18 Wanneroo Song Line	84	4.4 one way	2 hrs	Easy
19 Herdsman Lake	88	8.5 circuit	2 hrs 30 mins	Easy
20 Thomsons Lake	92	6.5 circuit	2 hrs	Medium
21 Yargan's Country	96	6 circuit	1 hr 30 mins	Easy

Walks at a glance

Café	Dogs	Ascent/descent	Highlights
Yes	Yes		St George's Terrace, city foreshore, West Perth
Yes	Yes		Botanic gardens, bushland, Federation Walkway
Yes	Yes		Funky cultural vibe, galleries and markets
Yes	Yes		A trip back to Colony days
-	Yes		Perfect Sunday afternoon family stroll
Yes	Yes		Industrial wasteland turned al fresco living
Yes	Yes		One of Perth's signature walks
Yes	Yes		Views across Matilda Bay to Perth CBD
Yes	Yes		Riverside picnics, swimming and fishing
-	Yes		Foreshore views out to the Swan River Basin
Yes	Yes		Views over Freshwater Bay to Point Resolution
-	Yes		The sleeping place of the Wagyl
Yes	Yes		Waterfront, fine views and fine food
Yes	Yes		Views of the Canning River, maybe dolphins
-	Yes		Heritage of early settlers' recreation
Yes	-		Walk, canoe, picnic, play golf, and see koalas
Yes	-		Limestone caves in Perth's most popular NP
-	Part		Heritage of the Coastal Plain's Mooro tribe
Yes	Yes		A rich and varied eco system close to the CBD
-	-		Wildlife reserve supporting over 10,000 birds
-	Yes		Aboriginal heritage and paperbark swamps

Walks at a glance

Walk	Page	Distance (km)	Time	Grade
Coastal Walks				
22 Guilderton Coastal Walk	102	5 circuit	1 hr 30 mins	Easy/medium
23 Mindarie Dunes	106	4 circuit	1 hr 30 mins	Medium
24 Trigg Mountain	110	4.3 circuit	1 hr 15 mins	Easy
25 Cottesloe Beach	114	4 one way	1 hr	Easy
26 Woodman Point	118	7 circuit	1 hr 45 mins	Easy
27 Cape Peron	122	2.7 circuit	1 hr	Easy
28 Rockingham Waterfront	126	5.6 return	1 hr 45 mins	Easy
29 Penguin Island	130	1.6 circuit	1 hr	Easy
The Darling Range				
30 The Echidna Trail	144	10.5 circuit	4 hrs	Medium/hard
31 John Forest Heritage Trial	148	10 one way	2 hrs 30 mins	Medium
32 Lake Leschenaultia Lakeside Walk	153	3 circuit	1 hr	Easy
33 Lake Leschenaultia Bush Walk	157	7 circuit	2 hrs	Medium
34 The Mundaring Weir Rail Trail	160	7 one way	4 hrs	Medium
35 The Golden Pipeline Trail	164	7 return	2 hrs 30 mins	Medium
36 Paten's Brook Track	168	9 circuit	3 hrs	Medium
37 Rocky Pool	172	4.7 return	1 hour	Easy
38 Lesmurdie Falls	176	2 return	20 mins	Medium
39 The Mason And Bird Heritage Trail	180	8 one way	2 hrs	Medium
40 Sixty Foot Falls	184	2 circuit	45 mins	Hard
41 Mount Dale Circuit	188	2.3 circuit	1 hr	Easy
42 Abyssinia Rock	192	10.3 return	2 hrs 30 mins	Medium

Walks at a glance

Café	Dogs	Ascent/ descent	Highlights
Yes	Yes		Beach walking, panoramic views, lighthouse
Yes	-		Extensive dunes and a long sandy beach
-	Yes		Climb Trigg Mountain and find the corkybark
Yes	Yes		A walk along Perth's favourite beach
-	Yes		Lovely summer's eve walk, BBQ or picnic
-	Yes		Islands, cliffs and bunkers - nature at work
Yes	Yes		History of the Rockingham area
-	-		Walk on the wild-side with the penguins
-	-	244 m	Enjoy a wide variety of wildflowers
Yes	-		Disused railway reserve, WA's only rail tunnel
Yes	-		Picnic, swim, and walk in this popular hills spot
Yes	-		Wildflowers, possums, bandicoots and echidnas
Yes	Yes	144 m	Old rail route to WA's first tourist destination
Yes	-	168 m	History of the Goldfields Water Supply Scheme
Yes	-	94 m	Re-growth forest and pine plantation, lake views
-	-		Jarrah forest and an idyllic rock pool
-	-	119 m	Waterfall, views over the Plain to Rottnest
-	-	156 m	Timber tramway, important conservation area
-	-	124 m	Ellis Brook cascades, 550 species of wildflowers
-	-	72 m	Views over the southern Darling Range
-	-	96 m	Explore granite outcrops on the Darling Range

Metropolitan Walks

At first glance the Perth Metro area might not seem a thrilling walking destination. Dismissed as being "dullsville" by many, the city is actually blessed with an idyllic location and a climate that makes outdoor living and recreation a practical reality. Alongside the seemingly perpetual blue sky is a natural beauty and varied and interesting history. Thanks to a network of dual use paths, an abundance of pristine parks and a push by local and state governments to encourage people to walk, the city provides a multitude of walking opportunities. The walks in this chapter are a small sample of what is available, but all are reasonably short so that they can be easily fitted into a hectic lifestyle; they are easy to get to and can be combined with other activities. I hope that you will be encouraged after doing them to go out and find more.

1 Perth City Walk

This walk takes you down St George's Terrace in the heart of the Perth CBD, along the Swan River Foreshore and back through Kings Park and West Perth. Along the way you will encounter some physical markers of the history of Perth from pre-European colonisation to the foundation of the Swan River Colony and on to the present day.

At a glance

Grade: : Easy
Time: 2 hrs
Distance: 6.7 km circuit
Conditions: Suitable all year round
Getting there:
Bus: CAT bus route to St George's Tce
Train: Perth Station
Car: Numerous car parks off St George's Tce and Hay St
Further Information:
www.perth.wa.gov.wa

1 Perth City Walk

Walk directions

1 The walk starts on the corner of King Street and St George's Terrace. Cross over and you will see the Old Perth Boys School, which dates back to 1854. It was designed by Colonial Secretary William Sanford and shows his passion for ecclesiastical architecture – indeed many people mistake the school for a church. The building is registered with the National Trust and is now home to Revely's Café.

2 On the corner of William Street and St George's Terrace is the Bank West Building. The colonial façade at the base of the tower block is all that remains of the Palace Hotel, built in 1885 at the height of the Gold Rush

1 Perth City Walk

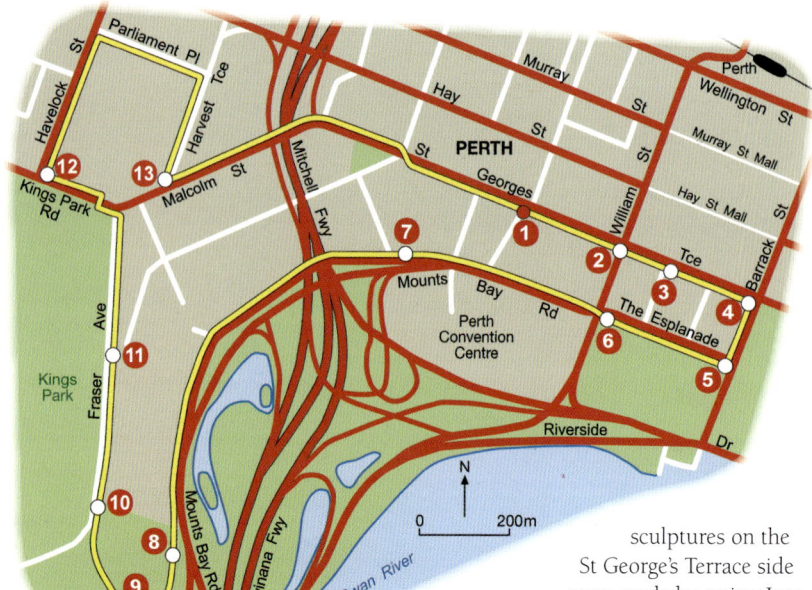

by John de Baun, and in its day considered one of the most elegant hotels in Australia.

3 Trinity Uniting Church has the most distinctive style of architecture among the churches in the city of Perth. Instead of being built in the gothic style that was popular at the time, Trinity Church was built in American Romanesque style by Henry S Trigg in 1873. It is the third church to have been built on the site; the second still remains and stands behind the present one. A little further up is the entrance to London Court. This mock Tudor reproduction of a London street was built in the 1930s by millionaire Claude de Bernales who made his money buying and selling mining equipment in the goldfields during the Great Depression.

4 Stirling Gardens is located on the corner of Barrack Street and St George's Terrace, and is the oldest public garden in Perth. Established in 1845 to be used as an acclimatisation garden for imported plants, the park was named after Sir James Stirling, founder of the Swan River Colony and the first governor of Western Australia. The current format of the gardens was built in 1965 with its Toodyay stone retaining walls and shallow pools. The Kangaroo sculptures on the St George's Terrace side were made by artists Joan Walsh-Smith and Charles Smith in 1997 and are a realistic representation of how kangaroos would have behaved in this area before colonisation. Less obvious are the Gumnut Babies in the flower beds on the Barrack Street side of the garden. These are based upon the characters Snuggle Pot and Cuddle Pie, created by May Gibbs in the 1930s. The sculptures were made in 2001 by Claire Bailey and Indra Geidens. Turn right into Barrack Street and walk down towards the river.

5 Turn right into the Esplanade. The large expanse of grass is the Esplanade Reserve and is used to host community, cultural and sporting events. Opposite the

1 Perth City Walk

reserve is the Lawson Building – a particularly fine example of art deco architecture.

6 Cross the Esplanade and walk past the bus station and the convention centre. The pyramid-shaped greenhouse is the Allan Green Conservatory, which was built in 1979 to provide a public facility where exotic tropical plants may be seen. Continue in a westerly direction along Mounts Bay Road.

7 On your right are the Bishop's Gardens. The house and the gardens were built in 1859 for Bishop Hale, the first bishop of Western Australia.

8 Keep walking past the Mount Hospital, the hotels and the King's Tower, and opposite the sign for Oldham Park you will see a turn off to your right. Go up it and look for the King's Park signpost, following the directions for the Kokoda Trail. The Swan River at this point is especially sacred to the

Trinity Uniting Church

1 Perth City Walk

Nyoongar people; in their dreamtime stories the Wagyl (a large snake like creature), which created the Swan River and the Darling Scarp, is said to have rested at this spot.

9 This is roughly the halfway point. The path you have been following brings you out at the bottom of Mount Eliza escarpment. Ahead is the Kennedy Fountain and on your right is a turn off going up some steps. The 150 steps, with a vertical rise of 62 metres, take you up Mount Eliza and are part of the Kokoda Trail Memorial which is a tribute to the Australian troops who fought in New Guinea from July 1942 to January 1943.

10 At the top of the hill, the path leads you past a rotunda. Turn right here and walk along the path that follows the edge of the escarpment. The State War Memorial is on your left and there are panoramic views out over Perth and the Swan River Basin. Mount Eliza was a very important site to the Nyoongar people: known as Mooro Katta, it was an important kangaroo hunting area and was also used for tribal gatherings. At the sign for the Aboriginal Art Gallery and the Kaarta Gar-up lookout, turn right and head up to Fraser Avenue, which is the main entrance road to Kings Park. Head for the City Exit, and as you do so you will pass the Queen Victoria Memorial on your right.

Bank West Building

11 The Bali Bombing Memorial commemorates the deaths of Western Australian tourists in the 2002 terrorist attack. Continue walking to the exit and the intersection of Fraser Avenue and Kings Park Road. Cross the road and turn left walking past Dumas House.

12 Turn right into Havelock Street and again into Parliament Place - at the end is Parliament House. Construction was commenced in 1902 and various extensions were added in 1958, 1964 and 1978. At the end of the street turn right onto Harvest Terrace.

13 At the end, turn left into Malcolm Street which leads into St George's Terrace. Shortly after walking under the

1 Perth City Walk

freeway you'll come across the Barracks Arch, the last remaining part of a barracks that was built in 1866 to house the Enrolled Pensioner Force, the guards on the convict ships coming to Australia. The main part of the building was demolished to make way for the Mitchell Freeway. After much public outcry the arch was reluctantly retained. By the arch is the statue of the Unknown Photographer which was made by Anne Neil in 1996. Carry on walking down St George's Terrace for approximately 600 metres to complete the circuit.

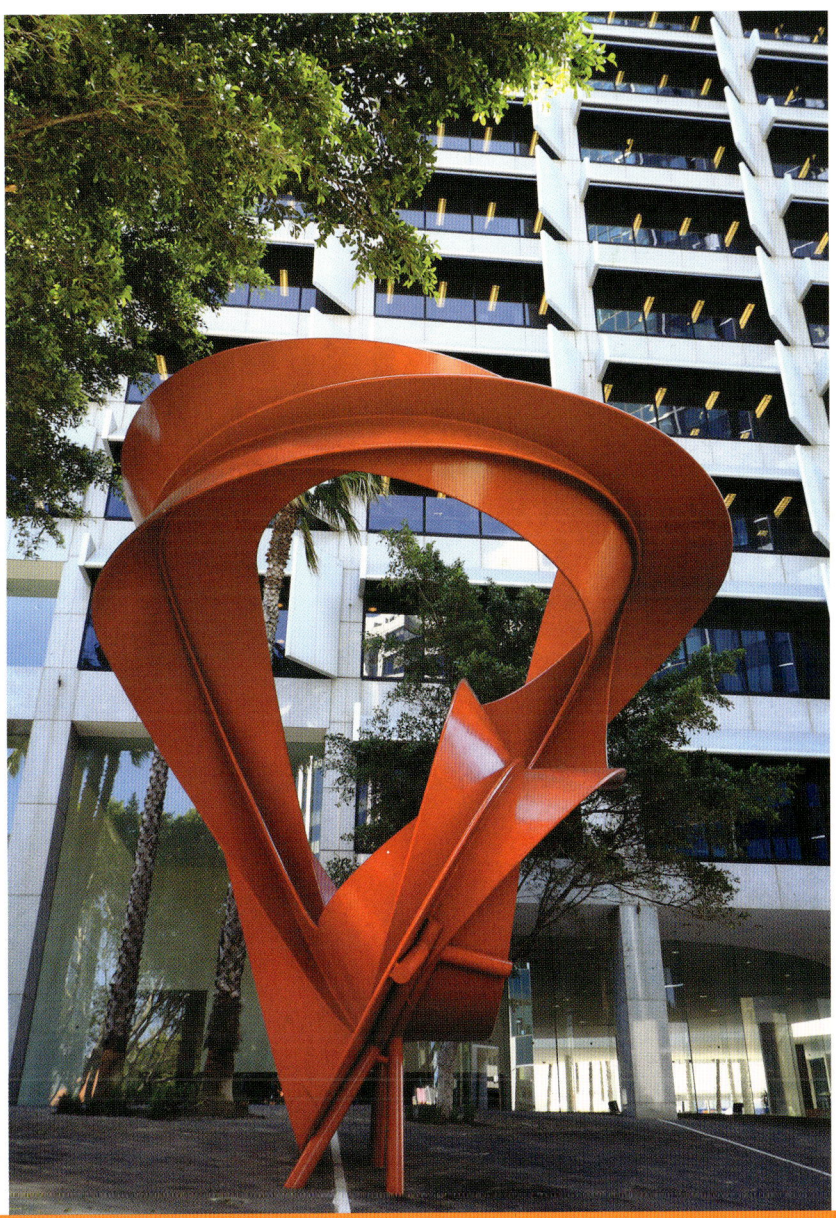

2 Kings Park Explorer

London has Hyde Park, New York has Central Park, Perth has Kings Park. With 4 square kilometres of natural bushland, it is the largest area of its kind to be found near the CBD of any Australian state capital. It is the city's pride and joy and this is reflected in the numbers of Perth locals who use it for recreation. This walk takes you through the Botanic Gardens (2,000 species of native plants within 17 hectares), on to the Federation Walkway (with its 222-metre long glass and steel elevated walkway through the tree tops) and then through native bushland that contains 291 different species of native plants. All of this is only a stone's throw away from Hay Street Mall.

At a glance
Grade: Easy
Time: 1.5 hrs
Distance: 7 km circuit
Conditions: All year round
Getting there:
Bus: The number 37 bus (39 on weekends) stops at the visitors centre
Car: Street parking near the park
Further Information:
www.bgpa.wa.gov.au, T 9480 3600

2 Kings Park Explorer

Walk directions

1 Start at the park's visitors centre, cross over Fraser Avenue to the entrance of the Botanic Garden and follow the signs for the Federation Walkway.

2 The Walkway is a masterpiece of design, the rusted steel of the pylons and the wooden decking blending in with the colours of the trees. The pylons have been decorated with subtle bush motifs that have been welded into the surface by artist Kevin Draper. The glass bridge is the centerpiece and it extends for 52 m between vertical pylons, its apex at 16 metres above the ground. At the end of the walkway turn left and follow the signs for Roe Garden.

3 Take the next left hand turn and eventually the path converges with Forest Drive. Turn right and head past the tram stop and the Roe car park until you see the Fire Fighters Memorial Grove. Cross over and walk up to the DNA tower.

2 Kings Park Explorer

4 Past the Tower walk down the Broadwalk, cross Lovekin Drive, continuing on to the Synergy Parkland. Walk through the park, past the café and around the lake, to May Drive, then cross and turn right onto the dual use path.

5 Past Kulbardi car park and the Saw Avenue picnic area turn-off, take the left hand fork of the junction. After nearly 300 metres there is another junction - go straight over and walk for another 200 metres before taking the right-hand turn.

6 Continue straight over at the crossroads and straight again through the Lotterywest family area. Pass the café and playground, cross over the road and follow the dual use path as it runs parallel to Kings Park Road.

7 Walk past the Pines Picnic Area and the Mt. Eliza Reservoir, following the path back to the visitor's centre.

Out and about – city walking

For those wishing to pavement-pound their way to fitness the City of Perth has put out its excellent brochure "Walking and Jogging Routes in the City of Perth". This brochure gives details of twelve walks that are all within easy reach of the Perth CBD and aims to encourage people to make walking part of their everyday fitness regime. For the more cerebral walker who wishes to combine their activity with a bit of history and culture the cities of Fremantle, Midland and Perth have put out brochures of themed walks. To augment the experience the City of Perth has also provided audio commentary that you can download to your iPod and listen to as you walk round.

3 Fremantle Culture Vulture Walk

Fremantle lies just 19 kilometres away from the Perth CBD and could therefore be assumed to be just another Perth suburb. In reality it is a village-city that is creative, open minded and relaxed. It has a distinctly Mediterranean feel, thanks to the Portuguese, Italian and Greek migrants who made it home, also has a very practical and down-to-earth side due to it being a working port with working class roots. An influx of hippies brought an alternative vibe late 1960s and early 1970s, and a major contribution has also been made by the artists, writers and musicians who have settled in Fremantle since its earliest days. This walk enables you to explore public artworks, galleries, artist studios and museums. You may want to purchase an arty crafty souvenir, it may inspire you to create your own works of art or it may just provide an enriching cultural experience. A walk through Fremantle's artscape could just provide you with all three.

At a glance
Grade: Easy
Time: 1 hr, up to a day if you visit all the art works, museums and galleries
Distance: 4.2 km circuit
Conditions: All year round
Getting there:
Train: Fremantle station
Bus: Fremantle Cat Bus
Car: Queensgate car park, the largest public artwork in the Southern Hemisphere
Further Information:
www.fremantletrails.com.au

3 Fremantle Culture Vulture Walk

Walk directions

1 The starting point is at the statue of Pietro Giacomo Porcelli by Greg James in Kings Square. The Square is for many people the social and cultural centre of Freo (as the locals call it). Bocce players can be seen playing along side street artists, tourists may rub shoulders with Italian matriarchs catching up on the latest news – a microcosm of daily Fremantle life. The Square is also host to the Village Art Market (www.villageartmarket.com, 1000-1600 daily, Oct-Apr) and there are several other artworks in the Square, so it is worth exploring before setting off.

2 Walk down the High Street and through the pedestrian Mall. As you do so you will pass the Mall Terrazzo, the Writers Walk Totems and numerous art galleries including the Adam Monk Gallery, Creative Native and Jarrahcorp Furniture and Fine Art. At the intersection with Cliff Street turn right and walk towards the harbour.

3 At the entrance to the Victoria Quay by the Fremantle Port Authority building there is a statue of C.Y. O'Connor by Pietro Giacomo Porcelli. It was O'Connor's engineering skills which enabled the port to develop. Nearby at the southern end of the E Shed is Southern Crossings by Tony Jones. The E Shed Markets are open on weekends only and have

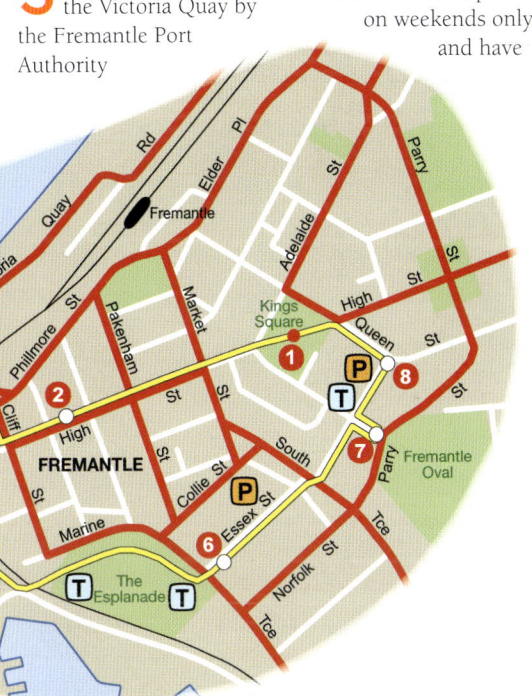

3 Fremantle Culture Vulture Walk

a variety of art and craft stalls. Turn left into Peter Hughes Drive and at the end is the Maritime Museum (0930-1700 daily except Weds). Outside the museum is the Welcome Wall which commemorates the contributions migrants have made to Western Australia.

4 Cross Slip and Fleet Streets leaving the Victoria Quay area and walk up past the pilot's cottages to the Roundhouse and Andrew Carter's Studio (1000-1730 Sat-Sun).

Kidogo Arthouse

5 From the Roundhouse go down the steps to street level and turn right following the dual use path that runs alongside the rail tracks. Stay on the seaside and as you walk towards the Fishing Boat Harbour you pass Kidogo Arthouse gallery and art school. Also nearby is the Shipwreck Gallery. On Bathers Beach is the Monument to the Old Jetty by Joan Campbell. At Fishing Boat Harbour opposite Cicerello's is the Bon Scott Memorial by Greg James. Another of James' pieces is close by – the Fishermen's Monument on the jetty – and it is quite interesting to watch how people interact with it if you while away some time at the nearby cafés. Cross the railway and walk across the Esplanade Reserve to Essex Street.

Mall Terrazzo

6 Walk up Essex Street to the Fremantle Markets on the corner of South Terrace and Henderson Street. The markets are a Fremantle institution and the range of goods on sale at the numerous stalls runs from fruit and vegetables to art and crafts (www.fremantlemarkets.com.au, 1000-1800 Fri-Sun).

3 Fremantle Culture Vulture Walk

7 Continuing up Henderson Street you reach the intersection with William Street. Turn right and follow William Street until the roundabout opposite Fremantle Oval, home to South Fremantle Football Club. On the roundabout is a statue of John Gerovich, commemorating his famous mark in the 1956 WANFL preliminary final over East Fremantle's Ray French. Turn back into Henderson Street and walk up to the intersection with Queen Street.

8 On the corner is the brightly coloured Queensgate Car Park. The car park was made over by Australian Centre for Concrete Art (AC4CA) artist Alex Spremberg. Turn left onto Queens Street and walk back to Kings Square.

Queensgate Car Park

4 Guildford Heritage Trail

Guildford was founded in 1829 and within a short space of time became a very important river port and trading centre. The town was laid out in the traditional English manner of the time – a central church, a village green and residential and commercial buildings surrounding them. Situated on the confluence of the Swan and Helena Rivers, Guildford is virtually an island and this has meant that the original colonial features of the town have largely been preserved – a visit can provide an insight into life in those far off times.

At a glance

Grade: Easy
Time: 1 hr
Distance: 3.8 km circuit
Conditions: All year round
Getting there:
Train: Guilford station
Car: Street parking and at the Tourist Information Office
Further Information:
www.swanvalley.com.au, T 9379 9400

This walk is a combination of the two walks the visitors centre have put together:-

- The Town Walk – 1,800 metres long following the red trail markers
- The River Ramble – 1,500 metres long following the blue trail markers

These have been combined into a figure of eight using the Visitors Centre opposite Stirling Square as the starting point. As you walk you will find interpretive panels providing historical details and interesting anecdotes about the town.

4 Guildford Heritage Trail

Walk directions

1 Start at the Visitor's Centre (formerly the Guildford Courthouse) at Stirling Square, on the corner of Meadow and Swan Streets), the starting point for Ensign Robert Dale's expedition to explore the Darling Range and the Avon Valley. Located conveniently next to it is the Colonial Jail where prisoners were held before being transferred to Fremantle by boat. Walk down Meadow Street following the red trail markers to the Post Office and cross the railway line at the crossing.

2 The town hall, with its art deco façade, is typical of the many public buildings that were built during the 1920s. Continue down Meadow Street, turning right into Helena Street.

3 Walk along Helena Street until it ends, turning right into Market Street and then immediately turning right again into Stephen Street.

4 At the end of Stephen Street turn right into James Street. If Fremantle has a coffee strip, Guildford has an antique strip - and this is it. It is quite fun to walk along and peruse the street front displays that are put out on fine days. By the burnt out shell of the Guildford Hotel cross James Street and the railway and head back into Stirling Square.

4 Guildford Heritage Trail

Taylor's Cottage

5 Follow the trail markers between the two church buildings and back to the Visitor's Centre.

6 At the Visitor's Centre follow the blue trail markers down Swan Street past the Rose and Crown Hotel. At the corner of the intersection of Swan and Terrace cross over to Padbury's Colonial Store and walk back down Swan Street.

7 Turn right into Meadow Street and walk towards the river, passing St. Charles Seminary on the way. Walk under the bridge to Moulton's Landing, the site of the original river port. Follow the path up onto the opposite side of Meadow Street and walk back down towards the square, passing Moulton's Cottage.

4 Guildford Heritage Trail

8 Turn right into Swan Street. This was the top end of town in the colonial era and some of Guildford's finest private residences were built here. At the Two Storey House cross over and walk for the final time back through Stirling Square. One of the key features of the Square is the Sugar Gums (*Eucalyptus cladocalyx*), the majority of which were planted between 1896 and 1901 and have become the "signature tree" of Guildford.

The Swan and Canning Rivers

The Swan River, with its major tributary the Canning, is a major defining feature for Perth and its suburbs. The entire river basin is one huge recreational playground attracting walkers, cyclists, picnickers, fishermen and boaters of all persuasions. It has also become one of Western Australia's most visited wine regions, with several cellar doors well worth the visit and many vintages well worth a sip.

5 John George Walk Trail

In 1829 Governor James Stirling took up 1,620 hectares of land in the Swan Valley, the estate extending eastwards from Guildford to the Darling Range, and southwards from the Swan River to the Helena River. He named the estate after his family home near Guildford in England. Between 1903 and 1934 land from the estate was purchased to create two housing subdivisions that were called West Midland and in 2001 the name was changed to Woodbridge. The riverside in Woodbridge has been a favourite spot with locals for many years. The John George Walk Trail links Woodbridge Riverside Park with the Reg Bond Reserve, it is perfect for a quiet day out with the family or just to walk the dog. There are wood BBQs in both parks.

At a glance

Grade: Easy, push chair friendly
Time: 1.3 hrs
Distance: 4 km one way
Conditions: Avoid walking in summer
Getting there:
Train: Woodbridge station
Car: Car park at Woodbridge Riverside Park on First Ave
Further Information:
http://tiny.cc/Woodbridge

5 John George Walk Trail

Walk directions

1 Starting in the car park, walk down to the waters edge and turn right. Cross the culvert and head past the large shed and the soccer pitches.

2 Cross over the wonderfully named Blackadder Creek on the wooden bridge and carry on past the warning signs about Tiger snakes and dugites.

3 When you come to another bridge, cross over and carry on through the picnic area.

4 As you walk along the river, you will see Caversham House on the opposite bank.

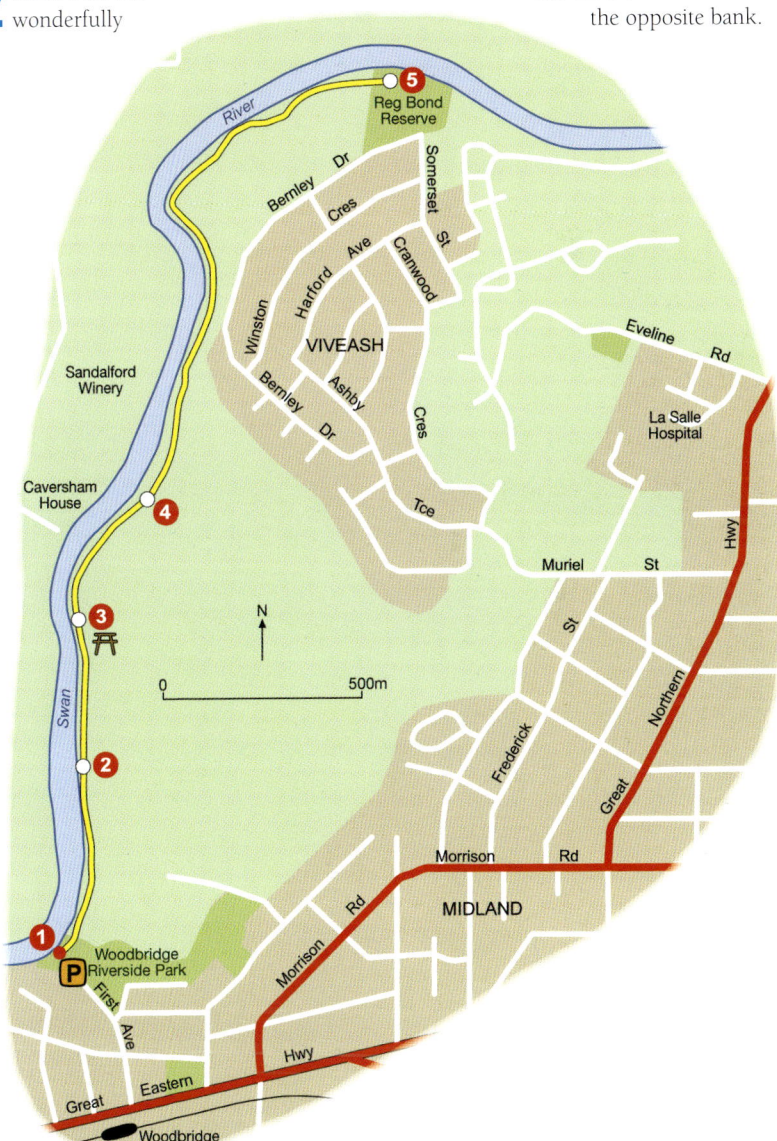

5 John George Walk Trail

This is a popular venue for weddings, and has its own private jetty. A few meters upstream is the Sandalford Vineyard which is one of Western Australia's oldest and largest privately owned wineries.

5 The path finally takes you into Reg Bond Reserve. To return to the start, retrace your steps or meet your arranged pick-up or second vehicle.

Perth environment – the Dugite

Dugite is the common name for *Pseudonaja affinis*, a type of Brown snake. Colour is not a good way to identify them as they can be grey, green or brown. The most distinguishing feature is that their heads are very small compared to the neck and it grades imperceptibly into the body. They can grow up to 2 meters long. Normally dugites are very shy and they avoid humans, however they are most active during the mating season of October to November. Their venom is one of the most lethal snake venoms in the world, but fatalities are rare with the last known one in 1993. Dugites are considered an endangered species and are protected under the Wildlife Conservation Act 1950 - to kill or injure one attracts a fine of up to $4,000.

5 John George Walk Trail

6 Claisebrook Cove

This walk takes you round much of the East Perth re-development on the banks of the Swan River. Most of this land was formerly used for industry and has now been re-claimed as parkland and housing developments. As you proceed around the walk you will gain an insight into the area's historical and spiritual significance to the Bibbulmun nation who lived here before the European arrival. There is also a substantial body of public art that commemorates the way people have interacted with the area. For those who would like a longer walk this could be combined with the East Perth trail to make a very pleasant 5.5 kilometre walk around this part of Perth.

At a glance
Grade: Easy
Time: 45 mins
Distance: 2.3 km circuit
Conditions: Suitable for all seasons, evenings are best in summer; suitable for pushchairs and wheelchairs
Getting there:
Bus: Yellow Cat bus stops outside Victoria Gardens on the corner of Royal St and Trafalgar Rd
Car: Car park at the entrance to Victoria Gardens

Standing stones on the Illa Kuri Track

6 Claisebrook Cove

Walk directions

1 Start in Victoria Gardens, just off Royal Street in East Perth, where there are toilet and picnic facilities. As you walk into the park you will see a large pedestrian footbridge straight ahead of you. This crosses the cove (and you will use it later). Just past the toilet block you will see two turn-offs on your left; take the second one and it will take you down to the river bank. Turn right and follow the river eastwards.

2 At the point where the Cove enters the Swan River is the Illa Kuri Track – a sacred dreaming path - which takes you past a series of standing stones which look out over the river.

3 At the end of the Illa Kuri Track follow the path round to the right and loop back to Victoria Gardens and this time cross over the bridge. Once over the bridge walk up Victory Terrace for about five minutes, after which you will see Tully Road on the left. Victory Terrace ends here but there is a path that heads northwards towards the Graham Farmer Freeway. Follow this and when you get to the fence turn right towards the river. Keep walking and you will find yourself almost under the Windan Bridge.

6 Claisebrook Cove

4 You are now at the top of Mardalup Park. Turn to your right and follow the riverside path southwards keeping the river on your left. The park contains quite a collection of sculpture which is worth looking at as it tells you something about the history of the area. You will soon pass a fishing jetty on your left which has views across the Swan River to the Burswood Resort.

5 At the southern end of the park there is a sculptural work called Concrete Poem by Robert Finlayson and PlanE, which marks the site of the old Perth Gas Works that used to be on this site.

6 The path follows the shoreline round to the right and takes you past Lamont's Restaurant and

6 Claisebrook Cove

the Holmes à Court Gallery before taking you under the bridge you previously crossed. Follow Henry Lawson Walk around the Cove, and as you do so you will see that the development here has a European feel with two and three storied houses fronting onto the river.

7 At the far end of the Cove is a small pedestrian bridge which crosses the water. Follow this and continue walking along the southern edge of the cove. There are a number of restaurants and cafés here, which are very popular at lunchtime with diners soaking up the al fresco ambience.

8 As you reach the bridge you will see the Trafalgar Road Culvert by Nola Farman, which

is one of the original trees from the area preserved in the installation. Follow the path to your right back up to Victoria Gardens where you began.

7 A Tale of Two Bridges

The Swan was originally named the Swarte Swaene-Revier by Dutch explorer, Willem de Vlamingh in 1697, after the famous black swans of the area. Vlamingh sailed with a small party up the river to around Heirisson Island. Governor Stirling's intention was that the name 'Swan River' would refer only to the watercourse upstream of the Heirisson Islands. All of the rest, including Perth Water, he considered estuarine and referred to as 'Melville Water'. The Government notice dated 27 July 1829 stated "...the first stone will be laid of a new town to be called 'Perth', near the entrance to the estuary of the Swan River". Almost immediately after the Perth was established, a systematic effort began to reshape the river and this continues today.

At a glance

Grade: Easy
Time: 2.5 hrs
Distance: 10 km circuit
Conditions: Good year-round walk
Getting there:
Public Transport: Esplanade train or bus stations
Car: Parking off Riverside Drive

On a beautiful warm spring day this walk epitomizes what living in Perth is all about. Fine weather with brilliant blue skies, the beauty of the river set against the backdrops of the city and the Darling Scarp. It all makes you feel lucky to live in such a great place. Successive state governments have been promising the "Dubai-ification" of the foreshore area for years and thankfully so far it has not happened. The walk can actually be started from three different locations:

- Barrack Street Jetty, Perth
- Mends Street Jetty, South Perth
- The Causeway

The only reason to choose one over the other is really to do with where you live and how you will travel to the start. It is also possible to split the walk in half and use the Swan ferry to return to the start if the 10 km proves too much.

7 A Tale of Two Bridges

Walk directions

1 Barrack Street Jetty is a strange place. It is separated from the CBD by parks and gardens yet it has an odd combination of tacky tourist attractions and sophisticated eateries. Most visitors either go to see the Swan Bell Tower and the Wheel of Perth, or to catch the ferry to Rottnest. To start the walk, follow the dual use path towards the Causeway.

2 After a long stroll along the shore, and just as Riverside Drive heads briefly inland, take the right fork in the path to Point Fraser (Boodjargabeelup in Nyoongar). Here you will find a large filtration system (for stopping pollutants from reaching the river) cunningly disguised as a garden with pond, reed beds and boardwalks.

3 A short way later, turn right up on to the Causeway. On the walk along here you pass Heirisson Island, which was first visited by Europeans in 1697 by Willem de Vlamingh. The island is home to a statue of the Nyoongar warrior Yagan, who was murdered by William and James Keates in 1833. Yagan was skinned and his head removed from his body, with both body parts kept as souvenirs. Yagan's head ended up in a

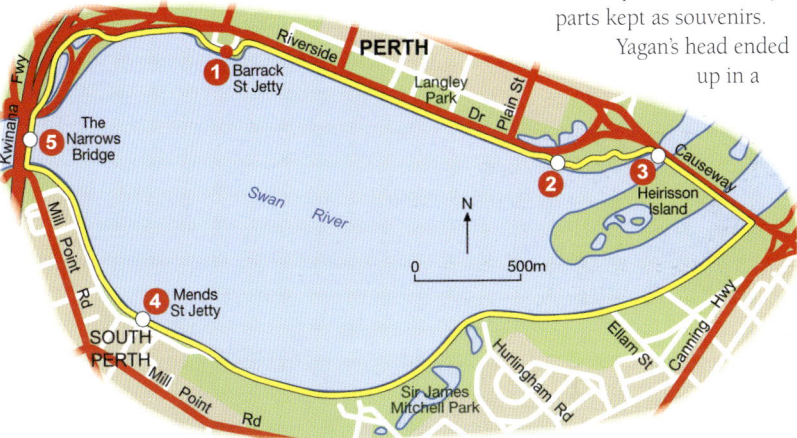

7 A Tale of Two Bridges

museum in England and after prolonged negotiations was returned to WA in 1997, though it has yet to be buried. Also on the island is a small colony of Western Grey Kangaroos. After crossing the Causeway turn right onto the dual use path, following the riverbank. This stretch is very popular with cyclists and walkers so to prevent any unpleasant confrontations the path has been separated to segregate walkers from cyclists.

4 After a further 4 kilometres of strolling through riverside parks you'll come to Mends Street Jetty - and if you want to cut short the walk you can return to Barrack Street Jetty via the ferry.

5 Otherwise, keep going up on to the Narrows Bridge. Use this to cross the river and on the other side follow the signs for Barrack Square.

8 Pelican Point - Matilda Bay

Like Point Walter on the southern banks of the Swan River, Matilda Bay is an incredibly popular recreational destination in Perth. People cycle, swim, fish, boat, walk, or just hang out in some of the most beautiful scenery in Perth. Known to the Nyoongar as Goodamioorup, Pelican Point was a special place because of the abundance of food and fresh water. Captain Mark John Currie RN was granted the land in 1829 and he modestly named it Point Currie. The property changed name and ownership several times until it was purchased in the 1870s by prominent businessman, and Perth's first mayor, George Shenton Jr. When Shenton passed away in 1910, Crawley Park Estate (as it was then known) was acquired by the state government and divided into land for the the new University of Western Australia and land for recreational purposes. During the Second World War the US Navy built a base for Catalan flying boats where the Mounts Bay Sailing Club now stands. Since the war the reserve was turned back over to recreational usage.

At a glance

Grade: : Easy
Time: 1.3 hrs
Distance: 4 km circuit
Conditions: Good year-round walk
Getting there:
Bus: Several bus routes stop at UWA on Mounts Bay Rd
Car: Park near the UWA boat shed on the corner of Hackett Dr and Mounts Bay Rd in Crawley

St John Lookout

8 Pelican Point - Matilda Bay

Walk directions

1 Starting in the car park by the University of Western Australia boat sheds, head to the dual use path that runs alongside Hackett Drive and follow it in a southerly direction.

2 Follow the path past the information boards and the café on the roadside path.

3 Cross Australia II Drive and follow the dual use path as it then snakes through the Matilda Bay Reserve and into J.H. Abrams Reserve.

4 Continue on to the boat ramp in the reserve, the most southerly point of the walk. Double back a short way then head onto the beach and follow the shoreline eastwards towards Pelican Point. Just before you enter the reserve, turn up to your left and take the faint path through the scrub and trees.

5 After 200 meters you come out onto the bottom section of Australia II Drive. Turn right and follow the road to the bird observation tower.

6 This tower looks out over a pond that is used by migratory waterbirds from Siberia and North Asia. There is an identification guide in the tower to help identify the many species that come here. When I was last there

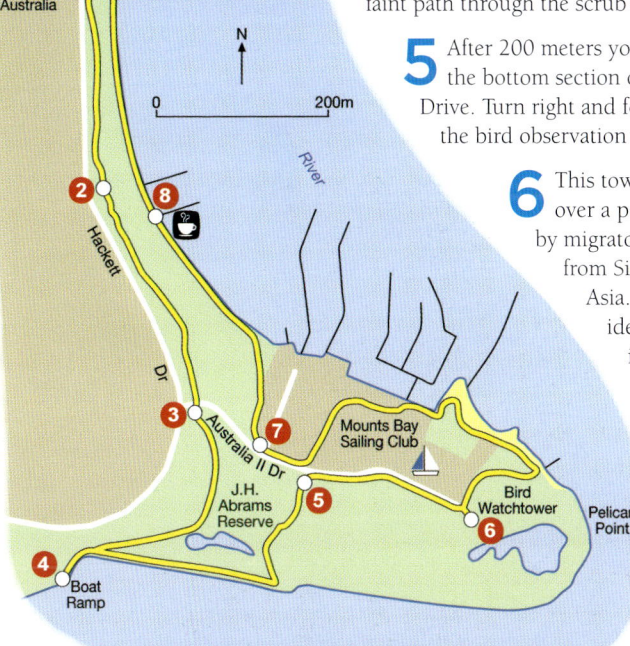

8 Pelican Point - Matilda Bay

I was fortunate enough to see a pair of Ospreys perching on some boat rigging. From the tower walk through Camp Cornwell, home of the Pelican Point Sea Scouts and down to their jetty. Turn left and walk back through the yacht club grounds, along the shore, then heading left up by the car park back to Australia II Drive. Turn right along the road, heading north.

7 After short way turn right off the road once more, walk past the DEC building on the riverside and then onto the beach. Veer to your left, keeping the shoreline to your right.

8 After about 500 metres you'll pass a café – a great spot to stop for a bit of refreshment – and from here it's about a kilometre back to the boat shed and the start of the walk.

9 Point Walter and Blackwall Reach

Known to the Beeliar as Jenalup, Point Walter was a place for women's business where they learnt essential skills, caught fish and foraged for native yams. Now it is one of Perth's premier family recreation areas as it is the perfect place for a picnic and BBQ. The scenic reserve has sweeping views over the river, and the beach is probably the most popular one on the Swan River. Blackwall Reach, named after a place in Greenwich London, is famous for its limestone cliffs. Commonly known as Blackies, people either come to climb its cliffs or jump off the top into the river below. Put simply Point Walter is the place where locals go on the weekends for a swim and a BBQ. For me a perfect summer Sunday morning would be to do the walk and then have breakfast at Walter's River Café.

At a glance

Grade: Medium
Time: 1 hr
Distance: 4.3 km circuit
Conditions: Year-round; involves some walking on sand and rocky surfaces
Getting there:
Bus: Nearest stop is 600m away from waypoint 2 on Beach St
Car: Parking at the end of Honour Ave, the continuation of Point Walter Rd off the Canning Hwy in Bicton
Further Information:
www.melvillecity.com.au

9 Point Walter and Blackwall Reach

Walk directions

1 Starting in the bottom car park follow the path up the hill, and at the top veer right to cross over the road. On your right is an information shelter and on your left is a gravel track, which follows the route of an old tramway. Follow that.

2 After about 700 metres, the track meets the pavement on Honour Avenue, continue south along it for a few meters then turn into the car park on your right. Look for some steps past the information shelter and these will take you to the Blackwall Reach Lookout, with views of Chidley Point, Mosman Bay and Freshwater Bay. Retrace your steps to the car park and just before the information shelter there is another track leading off on your left which takes you to another lookout.

3 As you leave the second lookout, just before the steps, there is a turn off to your left. Follow the trail and then turn left onto the dual use path. Now, depending upon the weather and the tide, you have two choices. If the weather is bad and/or the tide high, follow the dual use path north and at the end make your way to the Point Walter Jetty. In good conditions follow the dual use path for 50 meters and then on

9 Point Walter and Blackwall Reach

your left are some steps that take you down to the beach.

4 Walk along the beach until you get to the sandbar, if you have been able to walk along the beach you should be able to walk along the sandbar. Follow this around the point to the jetty.

5 At the jetty turn onto the eastward path and follow this past the café and through the car park.

6 The path meets Burke Drive as it intersects with Carroll Drive. Cross over the road here and follow the dual use path to your right that goes up the slope and between the trees.

7 Just before the path meets Honour Avenue, turn right and walk back down to where you started.

9 Point Walter and Blackwall Reach

Perth history - The Europeans Arrive

The first known European visitors to the Swan River were in a Dutch fleet commanded by Willem de Vlamingh. They landed at Cottesloe in 1697 and traveled eastwards as far as Freshwater Bay. They were not happy with what they found but named the river after the curious black swans they saw. In 1801 the French arrived under the command of Nicholas Baudin and they discovered the mouth of the Canning River at Applecross. Captain James Stirling and the British arrived late in 1827, and two years later returned to establish the Swan River Colony. Since then the river has been modified to aid settlement, with the process continuing to this day. There is precious little left of the original vegetation that originally fringed the river, and the course of the river and its wetlands have been substantially drained and altered. Despite this the river remains a haven for wildlife with fish, dolphins, turtles and waterbirds, both indigenous and migratory, calling it home.

10 Claremont Foreshore

Prior to European colonization the Claremont Foreshore was used by the Nyoongar for fishing and catching waterfowl, and it also had a source of permanent fresh water. In 1830 John Butler set up an inn at Freshwater Bay to service people travelling between Perth and Fremantle. From that time on land in the locale was quickly acquired by settlers and the townsite steadily grew. The community was named Claremont by a James Morrison after his wife Clara. This walk gives views across to Alfred Cove, Lucky Bay, Point Walter, Mosman Bay, and Freshwater Bay. The starting point at Jetty Road is the most convenient for people using public transport, but it can easily be walked in either direction.

At a glance

Grade: Medium
Time: 1.5 hrs
Distance: 5 km one way
Conditions: Not a winter walk; requires good weather and a low tide; some beach walking on sand and limestone rocks

Getting there:
Bus: Frequent bus services along the Stirling Hwy (10 mins walk)
Train: Claremont station (10 mins walk)
Car: Parking at both ends off Victoria Ave in Claremont

Further Information: www.claremont.wa.gov.au

10 Claremont Foreshore

Walk directions

1 Starting in Jetty Road, walk down to the Claremont Jetty. This was built in 1898 and was used regularly by passenger and cargo boats. Sheep were occasionally offloaded here and driven up Bayview Terrace to the Showgrounds. To your left is Claremont Yacht Club. Turn right to walk south along the foreshore.

2 As you pass the end of Chester Road you'll pass the site of the old Claremont Public Baths which were built in 1901 and remained in use until 1972. Continue to walk through the reserve.

3 Shortly you'll pass another reserve on your left: Mrs Herbert's Park. This is a dog exercise area and dogs may be let off the lead here. If you turn up through the park as a side trip you'll discover Claremont Museum. As you continue walking along the beach it becomes very narrow in places, and you need to watch your step carefully.

4 At the Bishop Road Reserve there is low lookout platform which looks a bit like a bunker and has views out to Point Walter and the Sandbar. Continue walking south along the foreshore until you see on your left the steps up Point Resolution Reserve.

5 Head up these to find the parking area marking the end of the walk. From here either retrace your steps or meet your pick-up or vehicle. As an interesting alternative (see over) you can walk through until you reach Victoria Avenue. Turn left onto the avenue and follow it all the way back to Mrs Herbert's Park, then head back down onto the foreshore where you turn right and so back to Jetty Road.

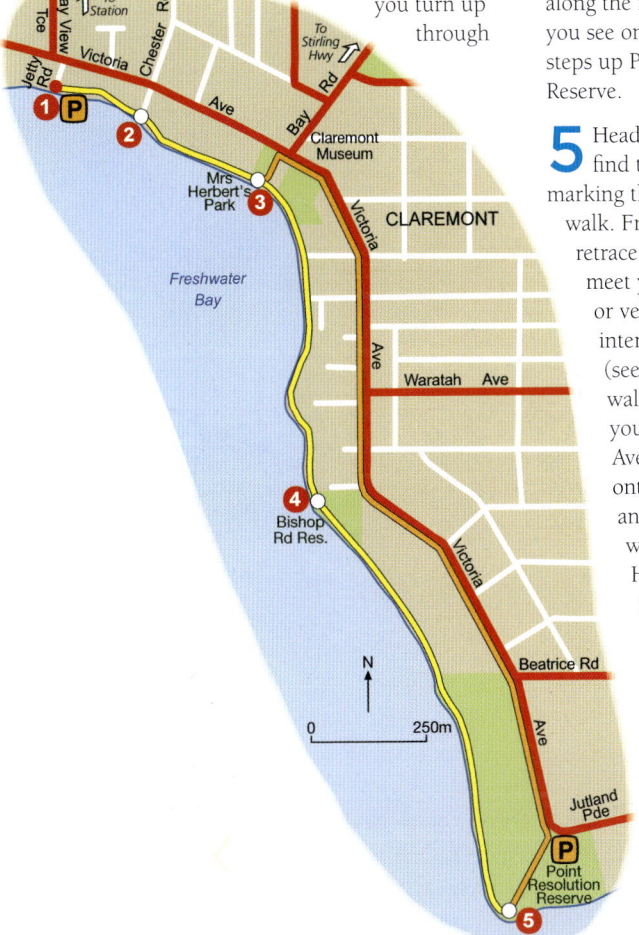

10 Claremont Foreshore

10 Claremont Foreshore

Perth history - Claremont Museum

One of the few remaining colonial era buildings left in Claremont, Claremont Museum was built in 1862 and was initially a school. By 1880 it had become the 'Appy 'Ome Boarding House. In 1898 it was acquired by the police and became the accommodation for one of the constables stationed at the Claremont Police Station. From 1906 to 1925 Freshwater Bay Police Station operated out of its front room. By 1973 it ceased to be used as it had been declared unfit for habitation. The building was then renovated and turned into a museum in 1975. The museum is open Monday to Friday 12 noon to 4 pm. The building sharply emphasises the contrast between the original colonial architecture and the modern 'mansions' you will see on your return stroll along Victoria Avenue.

11 Freshwater Bay

Peppermint Grove is one of Perth's most beautiful suburbs, with its tranquil tree-lined streets and lush verdant parks, and located by the calm waters of the Swan River. The suburb was so named because of the profusion of peppermint trees at the time of first settlement, some of which remain along the foreshore. This short walk has wonderful views out over the river across to Claremont and Point Resolution.

At a glance

Grade: Easy
Time: 45 mins
Distance: 2.3 km circuit
Conditions: Good year-round walk
Getting there:
Train: Cottesloe,
Bus: Buses stop on View St
Car: Parking on Lilla St and Hobbs Pl, Peppermint Grove
Further Information:
www.peppermintgrove.wa.gov.au

11 Freshwater Bay

Walk directions

1 From the car park on Hobbs Place, near the Royal Freshwater Bay Yacht Club, walk northwards down to the grassy area on the foreshore and turn left onto it.

2 As you walk you pass several Moreton Bay fig trees, which provide wonderful shade on hot summer's days. Just before the Old Tearoom Jetty the path divides, take the lower, right-hand branch. The Old Tearoom Jetty was built in 1901, was destroyed by a fire in 1980, and only the jetty was rebuilt. Continue walking past the Scotch College Boat Shed.

3 After another 500 metres or so, climb up the steps you'll come across to come to a junction. Take the left-hand turning and walk through the trees and up the cliff side. The top of the cliff affords some great views out over Freshwater Bay. It is amazing what a difference a slight rise in elevation can do for a view. From here take the path south again, parallel to the foreshore and adjacent to the Esplanade.

4 When you come to a fork in the path veer right and continue for 50 meters, to the point where the path goes to cross the Esplanade. Turn off the path to the left and walk down the slope on the grass, back to the foreshore.

5 Turn right and re-trace your steps back to Hobbs Place, stopping at the kiosk for refreshment if needed.

11 Freshwater Bay

Perth history - Derbal Yerrigan and the Dreamtime

In the dreamtime two rainbow serpents, or Wagyls, left what is now called the Avon Valley by following Derbal Yerrigan, or the Avon and Swan Rivers, down to Walyunga National Park where the female Wagyl laid some eggs, which are now the boulders in the rapids. They continued their journey down the Swan to Belmont where the male Wagyl shed some of his skin - the scales can be seen in the form of shells embedded in the riverbank. When they got to Melville they swam round and round with such force that they created a huge bay. The two Wagyls then had an argument and split up. She burrowed into the ground and headed south to re-surface at and creating Bibra Lake, and immediately also creating Yangebup Lake and Thomson's Lake. The male also burrowed deep into the ground, but he went north under Mount Eliza to create Lake Monger, Karrinyup Lake, Joondalup Lake and Yanchep Lake. After a while they got lonely so they reunited at Melville and their celebration at being together created Crawley Bay. The two Wagyls continued their journey down river to Fremantle and then out beyond Rottnest Island and back to the dreaming.

12 Rocky Bay - Garanup Park

When European settlers first arrived in Western Australia, if they wanted to get to Perth they had to disembark ship at Fremantle, ride or walk to Preston Point then cross the Swan River by ferry to Minim Cove and finally travel by bush track to the town. For much of the 20th century, heavy industry was located in this area, but after the Second World War there was a decline and many of the factories either closed down or re-located. In the 1960's archaeological discoveries found that Minim Cove was previously an Aboriginal tool-making site dating back some 10,000 years. Recently the land has undergone considerable rehabilitation and is now arguably one of Australia's most sought after addresses, the cliff-top location affording stunning views of both the Swan River and the Indian Ocean. The development has been carefully done, however, to allow public access to paths and a series of reserves so you do not have to live here to enjoy this beautiful location.

At a glance

Grade: Medium
Time: 1 hr 45 mins
Distance: 5.7 km return
Conditions: All year-round; predominantly on dual use paths, but involves some steps
Getting there:
Bus: Stops on Stirling Hwy
Train: The southern end of the walk is close to North Fremantle Station
Car: Car park off Hutchinson Ave, off McCabe St, Mosman Park
Further Information:
www.mosmanpark.wa.gov.au

12 Rocky Bay - Garanup Park

Walk directions

1 From the car park at the end of Hutchinson Avenue walk onto the dual use path and down to the bench that overlooks the bay. From here there are views of Preston Point and the East Fremantle Yacht Club.

2 By the gazebo there is a path that follows the cliff side down to a set of steps on your left. These steps go down to a small beach with a jetty. Head back up the steps and rejoin the path veering left. Follow this for about 700 meters until you find another gazebo with steps that go down to Milo Beach.

3 I spent twenty minutes here once watching a pod of dolphins playing in the bow waves and wakes of boats using the river. On the far side of the gazebo take the steps back up to the cliff top. Continue west along the dual use path for nearly a kilometre until it runs into Rule Street.

4 On your right-hand side at this point is Perth's old soap factory, which was operational up until 1959 and has since been converted into apartments. Walk along Rule Street a short way until you have the opportunity to veer left into the reserve. After 100 meters there are some steps. They do lead right down to Rocky Bay Beach, but halfway down is a short turn off that goes to a cave know as Kairp Ngun Gar in Nyoongar. The Nyoongar believe that in the dreamtime the Wagyl rested in this cave by coiling itself around the stone pillar in the center of the

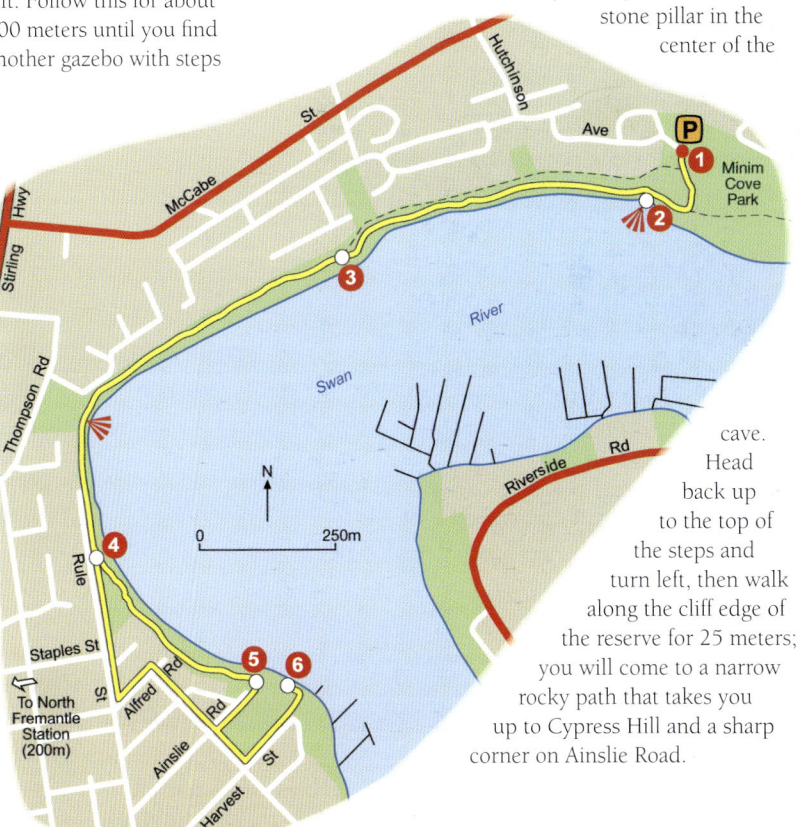

cave. Head back up to the top of the steps and turn left, then walk along the cliff edge of the reserve for 25 meters; you will come to a narrow rocky path that takes you up to Cypress Hill and a sharp corner on Ainslie Road.

12 Rocky Bay - Garanup Park

5 Take the left-hand direction along Ainslie Road, then turn left into Corkhill Street. A short while later turn left again into Harvest Street. On the left hand side of the Water Police building at the end there is a narrow path that goes down to the beach.

6 There are a couple of shelters with benches and tables here, plus a jetty and some steps down into the water. This is an idyllic spot for a swim on a summers day. Retrace your steps up Harvest Road and turn right back into Corkhill Road.

7 Pass the junction with Ainslie Road and continue to the end of the street. Turn left into Alfred Road and then right again into Rule Street. Walk along Rule Street until it joins the dual use path that you left at waypoint 4, then retrace your steps back to Minim Bay and Hutchinson Avenue.

13 From The River To The Sea

This walk can be done either direction either starting at the Beach Street Jetty or at South Beach. It is also a happy coincidence that there are excellent cafés at each end of the walk.

At a glance

Grade: Easy
Time: 2 hrs
Distance: 6.5 km one way
Conditions: Year-round walk; pushchair friendly
Getting there:
Bus: 103 bus stops at Fremantle Bridge
Car: Park at Beach Street Jetty, Fremantle
Further Information:
www.fremantletrails.com.au

13 From The River To The Sea

Walk directions

1 Start at the Beach Street Jetty car park and follow the dual use path out of the car park and under the Fremantle Bridge. After approximately 400 metres you will be at the entrance to Victoria Quay. Cross over here and continue down Beach Street until you reach the lights where you cross over.

2 Opposite Victoria Quay Entrance Gate #2, cross over the road and continue walking along the dual use path alongside Victoria Quay Road. Head under the railway bridge and follow the path through the harbour.

3 After about 1.5 kilometres, pass the E Shed Market on the

13 From The River To The Sea

waterfront side of the building then turn left and continue up Victoria Quay Road until you get to the entrance to the harbour at which point you can choose to visit the Maritime Museum (see below).

4 Veering left, pass the CY O'Connor statue, then turn right onto the dual use path just before the railway. This path continues directly to the Roundhouse. Follow the pathway to the Roundhouse.

5 The Roundhouse is the oldest remaining building in Western Australia. Built as a gaol between 1830 and 1831, it had eight cells and a gaoler's residence, which all opened up into a central courtyard. To visit the Roundhouse go up the steps. Entry is by gold coin donation. The adjacent Whalers Tunnel was constructed in 1837 by the Fremantle Whaling Company to allow the transport of whale oil between Bathers Bay the town. Interestingly, before European arrival, Bathers Bay was known as a place where whales (mimang in

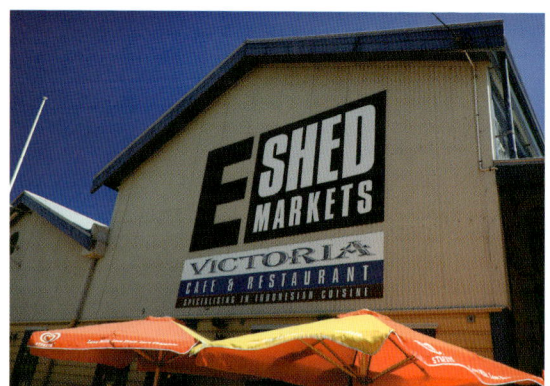

Out & about
– visiting the Maritime Museum and HMAS Ovens

If you want to visit the Maritime Museum and submarine HMAS Ovens (open 0930-0700, Thursday-Tuesday) continue south at waypoint 4 into the harbour. The museum and submarine are about 200 metres down here on the right-hand side. To rejoin the walk, retrace your steps to waypoint 4, turn right, pass the CY O'Connor statue, then turn right onto the dual use path just before the railway.

13 From The River To The Sea

Nyoongar) would beach and the local population would gather and feast on them. Head through the tunnel and turn left along the dual use path.

6 You'll soon see a fish and chip restaurant on your right and the Shipwreck Galleries of the Western Australian Museum on your left. The latter is open 0930-1700 Thursday to Tuesday (entry by donation) and houses various artifacts, including several remains and finds from the fascinating Batavia shipwreck. Continue south along the dual use path adjacent to Marine Terrace.

7 You'll now pass the Fishing Boat Harbour which offers plenty of places to stop for refreshment should the need prove too overwhlming. Keep heading south on the dual use path.

8 Walk past the Fremantle Sailing Club and carry on to South Beach. To return to your car catch the Freo CAT bus on Marine Terrace - the stop is opposite the Sealanes Building. This will take you back to the station where you need to catch the 103 bus to take you to Fremantle Bridge, and from there it is a short walk back to your starting point.

Perth history - Fremantle

On 25 April 1829, the ship HMS Challenger under the guidance of Captain Fremantle had arrived in the waters off the Fremantle coast to make preparations for the Swan River Colony. On 2 May 1829, Captain Fremantle formally took possession of the entire west coast of New Holland on behalf of King George IV in a ceremony conducted just near the south head of the Swan River. A few days later a camp was set up in a bay just south of the head, and Fremantle has been occupied ever since. A month later, on 1 June, Captain James Stirling on the Parmelia arrived to officially set up the Swan River Colony. The settlement of Perth began on 12 August 1829. Captain Fremantle left the colony on 25 August after providing much assistance to Stirling in setting up the colony. It was then that Stirling decided to name the port settlement 'Fremantle'.

14 Deep Water Point

Deep Water Point is a very popular recreational area situated on the Canning River between the Canning and Mount Henry Bridges. This walk can basically be divided into two sections: the eastern bank of the Canning, which is now being set aside for heritage and nature conservation, education and passive recreation values; and the western bank, which is given over to housing and active recreational activities such as water skiing, rowing, and fishing. A variety of wildlife can be observed while walking along this stretch of the river, the most notable being bottlenosed dolphins and osprey. In summer, when the water is more saline, bottlenosed dolphins can be seen swimming under the Mount Henry Bridge. They drive shoals of fish into shallow water or onto the river banks to facilitate catching them. The osprey, or fish hawk, currently nesting on the Mount Henry Peninsula is a fairly permanent resident of the area, nesting on a platform and post donated by Western Power after a fire swept through the bush here in late 1997. An ideal scenario would be to do the walk on a balmy summer's evening and have a picnic or BBQ at the starting point afterwards.

At a glance

Grade: Easy
Time: 2 hrs
Distance: 8 km circuit
Conditions: Year-round walk; push chair friendly
Getting there:
Public Transport: Canning Bridge Rail Station and Bus Interchange (then start at waypoint 3)
Car: The Esplanade is just off Canning Highway on the Applecross side of the Canning Bridge
Further Information:
www.melvillecity.com.au;
www.southperth.wa.gov.au

14 Deep Water Point

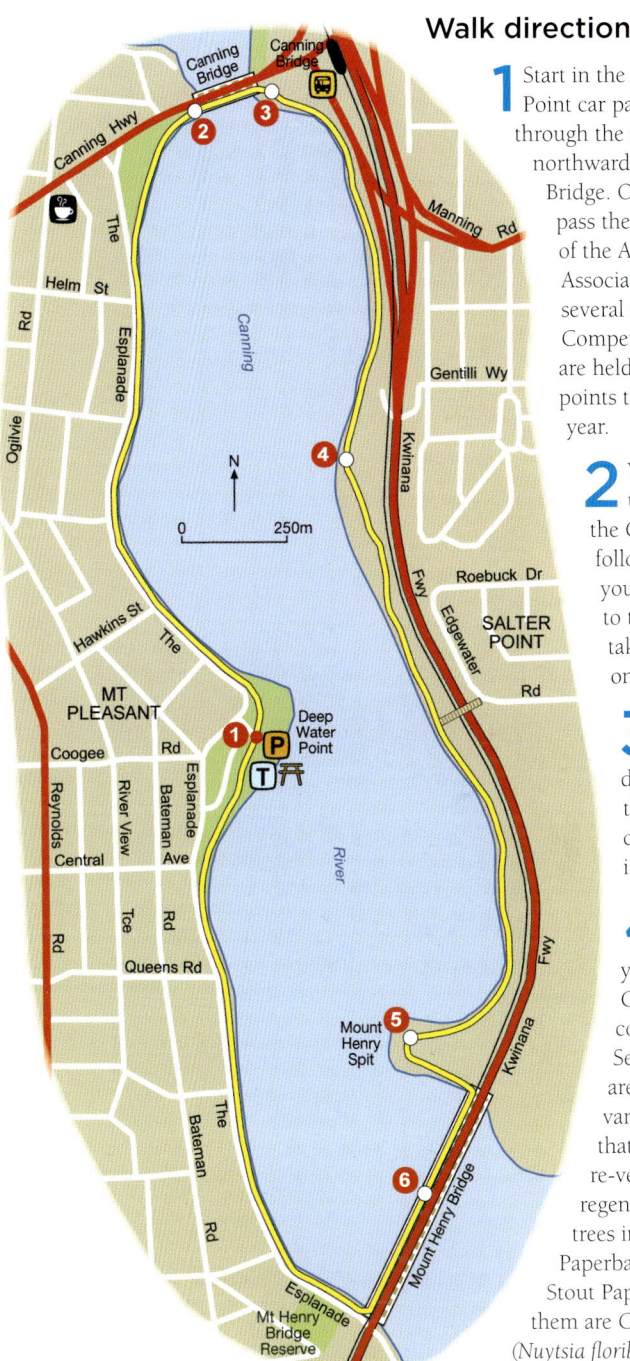

Walk directions

1 Start in the Deep Water Point car park and walk through the reserve heading northwards towards Canning Bridge. On the way you'll pass the Headquarters of the Amateur Rowing Association of WA and several rowing clubs. Competitions and regattas are held here at varying points throughout the year.

2 When the dual use path meets the Canning Highway, follow it round to your right to get to the bridge, then take the left fork up onto it.

3 At the far end of the bridge drop back down to the foreshore and continue following it south.

4 After just over a kilometre you'll come to the Cloisters Foreshore conservation area. Several schools are involved in various projects that contribute to re-vegetation and regeneration here. The trees include Freshwater Paperbarks and the rarer Stout Paperbarks. Amongst them are Christmas Trees (*Nuytsia floribunda*), semi-parasitic trees that produce bright

14 Deep Water Point

orange flowers over the Christmas period. This is said to be the largest parasitic plant in the world.

5 About two kilometers further on is Mount Henry Spit. Walk through the reserve and along the beach to access Mount Henry Bridge via some steps. If you have children in a pushchair, continue along the dual use path for easier access to the bridge. Pelicans, coots, cormorants and ibis can be seen here.

6 Cross Mount Henry Bridge. The name comes from Lieutenant John Henry of HMS Challenger, who led the expedition to explore the Canning River's headwaters in 1829. After crossing the bridge veer to your right to walk through the park, then cross the road and turn left onto the dual use path at the jetty. It is a little less than a two-kilometre walk along the foreshore back to Deep Water Point.

14 Deep Water Point

Perth history – the Great Depression

During the Great Depression of the 1930s, unemployment in Australia hit 25% and many of the unemployed were made homeless. The Cloisters Foreshore became a shanty town for the unemployed. When families first started arriving the police supplied them with small tents as it was supposed to be a temporary measure. Over time this assistance changed and new arrivals were given old oil drums with which to build more substantial dwellings. It is possible to read Shirley Burns' account of growing up here in her book *The Camps at Canning Bridge: during the depression years 1930-1933*

15 Woodloes Walk

The Canning River, known as Dyarlgaard to the Beeliar people, was an important summer hunting ground. However, when the Europeans arrived in the 1830's the land usage and management changed considerably and evidence of that change can be seen as you walk around. The walk through Canning River Regional Park starts at Mason's Street Landing which was once the site of the timber mill and landing for the Mason and Bird Timber Company. From this landing timber felled in the Darling Ranges was transported by barge to Fremantle for export. (For more information on the Mason and Bird Timber Company see the Mason and Bird Heritage Walk.) Over time the banks of the Canning River became firstly farmland and then suburban housing. The river has always been a popular recreational place and fishing, boating, walking and swimming were all popular with the early settlers and remain so to this day.

At a glance

Grade: Easy
Time: 1 hr
Distance: 4 km circuit
Conditions: Year-round walk; push chair friendly
Getting there:
Bus: Regular services down Albany Hwy
Car: Parking on Liege St, just off Albany Hwy in Cannington
Further Information:
www.canning.wa.gov.au

15 Woodloes Walk

Walk directions

1 Start in the Mason Street Landing car park off Liege Street and walk south through the park until you are forced to exit at River Road. Walk a short way up here then right onto Woodloes Street. Follow this and you'll soon pass Woodloes Homestead and Museum.

2 The museum is open to the public - contact the City of Canning on T 9231 0606 for opening times. The homestead was built in 1874 for Francis Bird, timber industry pioneer and architect, and had the distinction of being the first architect-designed dwelling south of the river.

Continue to the end of Woodloes Street and turn right onto the dual use path that runs alongside Nicholson Road.

3 Cross over the Canning and shortly after turn right onto another dual use path. A lot of the original farmsteads have been cleared for housing, some acquired to create the Canning River Regional Park, but in places traces of them remain. This can be seen in the plants that farmers have left behind: citrus, mulberry and olive trees, taro, blackberries, arum lilies and canna lilies. Continue along the path through the park until you come to another bridge.

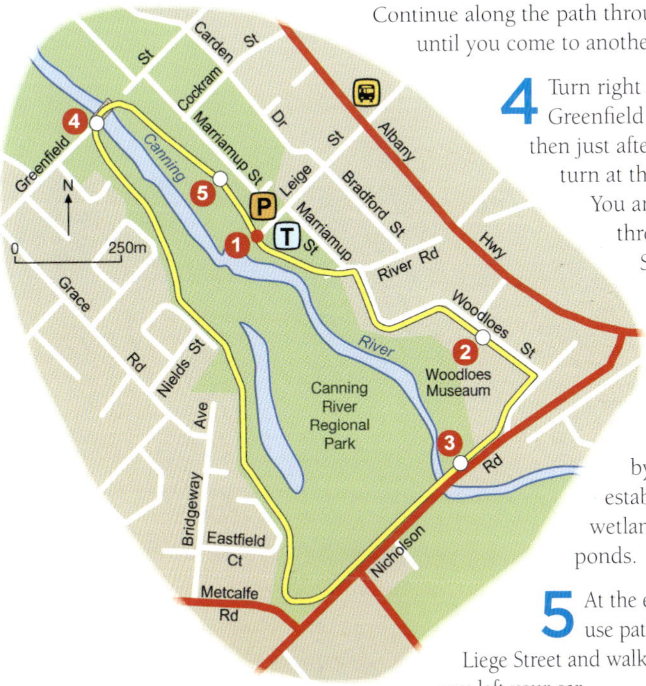

4 Turn right and cross the Greenfield Street Bridge, then just after take the right turn at the T-junction. You are now walking through the Liege Street Wetland project. The Liege Street water catchment is being improved by the re-establishment of wetland reed beds and ponds.

5 At the end of the dual use path turn right onto Liege Street and walk back to where you left your car.

73

15 Woodloes Walk

15 Woodloes Walk

Perth history – the Canning River

The first European contact with the Canning River was in 1801 when Nicolas Baudin's French exploration party spotted the mouth and subsequently named it Entrée Moreau after Charles Moreau, a midshipman with the party. The Canning River received its contemporary name in 1827 when Captain James Stirling aboard the HMS Success, following an examination of the region in March 1827, named the river after George Canning who was Prime Minister of Great Britain at the time and whose government facilitated the funds for the expedition.

Wetlands

The Swan Coastal Plain is the land formation lying directly west of the Darling Scarp and it contains the Swan River. Traditionally this area was inhabited by the Yued, Whadjuh, Binjareb and Wardnai Nyoongar people. On the plain is an extensive belt of wetlands that has been widely acknowledged as a biodiversity hot-spot having a greater number of endemic species than most other regions in Australia. Within this the Nyoongar, with their hunter-gatherer life-style, managed the land with their fire-stick farming and survived by hunting and trapping a variety of game, including kangaroos, possums and wallabies; by fishing using spears and fish traps; as well as by gathering an extensive range of edible wild plants, including wattle seeds. Since European colonization three-quarters of these wetlands have been drained for urban development. What remains has suffered unknown but certainly extensive damage through the introduction of feral animals and plants. Thankfully Australia is a signatory of the Ramsar Convention and several key wetlands on the Swan Coastal Plain have been set aside for conservation. Around the Perth Metropolitan Area the wetlands can be split into two distinctive areas:

- The Beeliar Wetlands are a chain of twenty six lakes stretching from Manning Lake in Hamilton Hill to Madura Swamp near Mandurah.
- The Great Lakes District which originally was a series of lakes stretching up to 50 kilometres north of the Swan River. Many of these have now gone e.g. Lake Kingsford is now Perth Railway Station, Lake Irwin is the Perth Entertainment Centre and Stone's Lake is now Perth Oval.

The walks in this chapter are great walks in and of their own right, but they also give the chance to explore the native flora and fauna of the Perth area and its significance to the original Nyoongar inhabitants.

16 Yanchep Wetlands Walk Trail

This trail takes you through the heart of the coastal wetland circumnavigating Loch McNess.

At a glance

Grade: Easy
Time: 45 minutes
Distance: 2.6 km circuit
Conditions: Good year-round walk; pushchair friendly
Getting there:
Bus: Bus stop on Yanchep Beach Rd
Car: Yanchep National Park access is off the Waneroo Rd; vehicular park fee of $11
Further Information:
www.dec.wa.gov.au

16 Yanchep Wetlands Walk Trail

Walk directions

1 Start at McNess House and walk down to the waters edge where you'll see the jetties for the hire boats. The trees on the banks are flooded gums (*Eucalyptus rudis*). Turn right and follow the path around the edge of the lake.

2 Soon after passing the Yanchep Inn (built in 1936 in a mock Tudor style) you'll come to a broad walk that will take you into the reed beds. Marron live in the shallow waters here and were a popular bush food. Fringe lilies (tjunguri in Nyoongar), with their attractive purple flowers, can be seen climbing over other plants. The lily produces tubers, a much thickened underground part of a stem or rhizome which serves as a food reserve and bears buds from which new plants arise, this also was an important item of bush tucker and was eaten roasted like a potato.

3 The path takes you over a small bridge and beside it are parts of the dredger that the sustenance workers in the 1930s used to dredge the lake. The money for these works was donated by Sir Charles McNess and this is why nearly everything in the park is named McNess. A bit further on is the turn off for the Ghost House Trail, but keep following the path round the lake.

4 At the southern end of the lake the banks are thick with sedges and rushes.

5 As you pass through the Lakeside Picnic Area it is possible to see some of the many species of ducks that inhabit the lake. The most unusual of these is the musk duck (*Biziura lobata*), which is very un-duck like in its looks and behaviour. It's blackish brown in colour and it sits very low in the water. If they feel threatened they submerge so that only their eyes and nostrils are visible. In the breeding season the males give off a very strong odour hence the name. McNess House is another 300 metres further on.

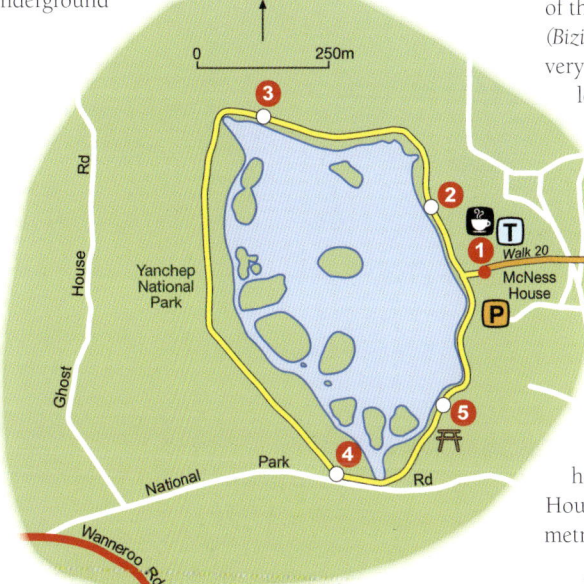

Yanchep National Park

The coastal plain during the pre-European era was an incredibly important environment for the Nyoongar people. The chain of lakes meant that there was abundant food and water all year round. The bullrush (yandjip in the Nyoongar language) was a staple food and its harvest was an important event which provided the opportunity for large social gatherings. The European corruption of the word yandjip gave Yanchep its name. Archaeological evidence shows that there has been Nyoongar habitation around Loch McNess (Wagardu as it was known) for about 6,500 years. The lake and the caves that are also in the park held particular significance, the lake being inhabited by the Rainbow Serpent and the caves by the Jinlan.

In 1905 2,283 hectares of land was set aside for preservation and Yanchep became one of Western Australia's first national parks. In 1994 the park was extended and upgraded and it has become one of WA's most visited national parks. People go to the park to walk the many trails, canoe, see wildflowers and koalas, to visit the limestone caves, picnic and play golf. There are in total nine walks in, or that begin in Yanchep and these are:-

1. Yanchep Caves Walk
2. Cockatoo Walk Trail
3. Yanchep Rose Walk Trail
4. Woodlands Walk Trail
5. Dwerta Mia
6. Wetlands Walk Trail
7. Ghost House Walk Trail
8. Yaberoo Budjara Heritage Trail
9. Coastal Plain Walk Trail

The descriptions here cover the Caves Walk Trail and the Wetland Walk. For more information about the others consult DEC's excellent brochure Wild About Walking - Yanchep National Park and Beyond which is available from the park's visitor information centre.

17 Yanchep Caves Walk Trail

This walk takes you through the bushland to the northeast of Loch McNess to Crystal and Cabaret Caves. At Crystal Cave it is possible to take a tour that will tell you how the caves were formed and some of their history. Should you wish to do so you will need to book a tour at the McNess House Visitor Centre and then time your walk to coincide. Cabaret Cave is no longer open to the general public but it is possible to book the cave for a subterranean dinner function!

At a glance

Grade: Easy

Time: 1 hr 30 mins, excluding cave tours

Distance: 4.5 km circuit

Conditions: Good year-round walk

Getting there:

Bus: Bus stop on Yanchep Beach Rd

Car: Yanchep National Park access is off the Waneroo Rd; vehicular park fee of $11

Further Information:
www.dec.wa.gov.au

17 Yanchep Caves Walk Trail

Walk directions

1 Start at the visitor centre and walk towards the tearooms. On your right are the information signs for the various walks. Initially all the walks start here and follow the same path.

2 After about 150 metres the trail heads off to the right. However, for a diversion to see the Koalas, the entrance to the Koala Broadwalk is bit further on your left.

3 When you reach the edge of the footy oval, take the right-hand fork in the trail and follow the markers for about 200 metres until you reach a vehicular road.

4 Turn left onto the road and walk for 30 metres, then take the right turn onto the path.

5 In about 200 metres you'll reach Crystal Cave. The Nyoongar did not generally enter the caves, as they believed that they were inhabited by evil spirits called Jinlan. The first European to see the cave was Henry White, a local pastoralist, in 1903. The path continues to the right of the ticket booth.

6 When the trail intersects with the Dwerta Mia Trail, keep heading straight on.

7 When the path crosses The Ghost House Walk and the Yanchep Rose Walk, take the left turn and you will very quickly reach Cabaret Cave.

8 Walk 120 metres from the cave entrance along the road. Watch out for and take a small trail that goes up a bank on your left and into some trees.

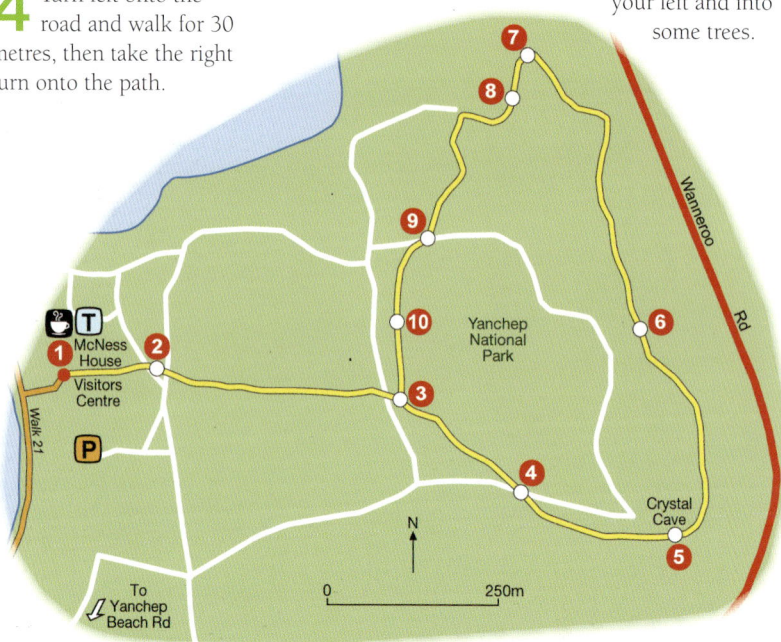

17 Yanchep Caves Walk Trail

9 At the next junction in the path, turn right and continue until you come to the information board for the Dwerta Mia. The path continues past a small bench and then turns left into the trees. A few metres further on and it crosses the road to Gloucester Lodge. Continue heading south.

10 Walk around the edge of the oval until you reach the road crossing. Cross over and follow the path back to McNess House.

18 Wanneroo Song Line

The area around Lake Joondalup was very important to the Mooro tribe of the Nyoongar people. The Yaberoo Budjara Heritage Trail (which translates as the land of the people of the north of Perth) traces the tribe's movement track that linked the linear lakes of the Swan Coastal Plain. The whole trail is 28 kilometres long, stretching from its start at Neil Hawkins Park to its end at Yanchep National Park. This walk just traces a small section of the beginning of the trail.

At a glance

Grade: Easy
Time: 1 hr
Distance: 4.4 km one way
Conditions: Not recommended in summer - push chair friendly
Getting there:
Train: Joondalup rail station
Bus: Stops in Boas Ave and Burns Beach Rd
Car: Parking off Boas Ave in Joondalup
Dogs: Not allowed in Neil Hawkins Park but allowed on dual use path
Further Information:
http://tourism.heritage.wa.gov.au

18 Wanneroo Song Line

Walk directions

1 The starting point is the statue in the picnic area of Neil Hawkins Park. Walk to the jetty and turn left onto to the dual use path. As you walk along the lakeside you can see the transition in the vegetation as it changes from tuart, banksia and zamia on your left to melaluca, reeds and sedge on your right.

2 After about 600 metres, take the turn off on your left to walk up to the lookout, which has views out over Lake Joondalup (the 'lake that glistens'). As you leave the lookout, instead of taking the path that brought you up, take the path on the right that leads down the slope. You'll see your earlier path join on the right, but ignore that and stay on this path as it veers gently around to the left to continue close the foreshore heading north.

3 In the undergrowth on your left you will pass some caves, but unfortunately they were damaged and rendered unsafe to enter when early settlers tried to drain the lake using them. In the dreamtime Malup Island (one of the lakes islands) was a sacred place, but a woman ignored this and went there. The Waugal (Rainbow Serpent) angry at her disobedience punished her by dragging her away through the caves to the sea.

4 After another 300 metres or so there is a bench under some peppermint trees (*Agonis flexuosa*). I always find the scent of these trees to be soporific and so it is a perfect place to sit and have a rest. The open forest next to the lake provides an abundance of food for

18 Wanneroo Song Line

Kookaburras - snakes, lizards, small birds, rodents, and insects. These birds are such a feature of the Western Australian bush that it is hard to believe that they were introduced to WA in 1897 from the Eastern States.

5 About 300 metres after leaving the bench, look out for a right turn down to the lake shore, a return side-trip of about 800 metres. The ground gets waterlogged by the lake so this may not be passable after heavy rains. After returning to the main path, carry on walking north along the dual use path for about two kilometers.

6 At the end of the walk either retrace your steps to Boas Avenue or walk up to Burns Beach Road and catch a bus (390, 391, or the 468) to Joondalup Station.

18 Wanneroo Song Line

Perth history – Bibbulmun statue

The woman in the statue is a Bibbulmun Yorga, meaning she is a woman from the people who come from the hills country that follows the coastline. She wears the kangaroo skin cloak (or buka) traditionally worn by the Nyoongar people. It normally consisted of the whole skin of two to three kangaroos sewn together, with the tail hanging at the bottom of the cloak. The cloaks were also used as rugs to sleep on at night. She is holding a yandi or wooden dish that is used for carrying wood, food, water, small babies and fire. The dingo is Dwerda the totem for the Waneroo, Yanchep and Moore River area

19 Herdsman Lake

Herdsman Lake (Ngurghboro in Nyoongar) is a lake that nobody knew what to do with. Originally called Great Lake by John Septimus Roe, who suggested it could be used for Perth's water supply, by the turn of the 20th century it had become Herdsman Lake and the Roman Catholic Church owned it and the surrounding land. After the First World War it was turned over to the Soldier Settlement Scheme and In 1921 there was an attempt to drain it, but this failed and the land was then used for grazing and market gardening. In 1936 there was a proposal to use the land for an airport, and by the 1960s it was to be used for housing. Luckily, common sense eventually prevailed and in 1999 Herdsman Lake was declared a regional park.

At a glance

Grade: Easy
Time: 2 hrs 30 mins
Distance: 8.5 km circuit
Conditions: Not recommended in summer when most of the lake is dry
Getting there:
Bus: 98 bus stops on Flynn St
Car: Herdsman Lake Wildlife Centre is at the end of Selby St off Flynn St
Further Information: Wildlife Centre: www.wagouldleague.com.au

The lake is only 6 kilometres from Perth's CBD, yet it is one of the best birdwatching areas for waterbirds in the Perth region. Attractions within the park include the Olive Seymour Broadwalk, Lake Herdsman Wildlife Centre, and Settler's Cottage. I have chosen to start the walk from the Wildlife Centre at the southern end of the lake, but a good alternative for those living north of the lake would be the reserve near the intersection of Selby Street North and Jon Sanders Drive.

19 Herdsman Lake

Walk directions

1 Starting in the car park of the Wildlife Centre head back down Selby Street toward Flynn Street and turn right onto the dual use path. Cross the bridge then turn right onto another dual use path immediately on the other side. Follow the path through the lakeside park, following the foreshore.

2 When you come to a playground there is an information board listing the fauna that lives on and around the lake. Continue on the path as it wends around the lake.

3 On the western fringe of the lake the main path veers away to the left, close to Halcyon Way. Turn right onto the bitumen path. The reeds and melalucas close out views of the open water and create a swamp environment.

4 Walk past the turn off for the Settlers Cottage Art Studios and follow the signs for Popeye Lake Park. You will find yourself walking parallel to The Foreshore road.

5 Housing subdivisions come virtually to the lake side here. Just off shore is an island with a sculpture on it, and behind that is a large fallen tree which is very popular roosting place for white ibis (*Threskiornis aethiopicus*).

19 Herdsman Lake

6 The path (now bitumen again) runs briefly alongside Parkwater Gardens. Before the path reaches the end of the road, take the right fork over the bridge to a T-junction. Turn left, and shortly after veer right at a fork. This path quickly meets the foreshore which you then follow around the northern end of the lake, passing through Popeye Lake Reserve. Continue following the foreshore until the path turns away from the water, alongside an area of bush, and up to the road.

7 Turn right onto the dual use path that runs along Jon Saunders Drive, walk for about 200 metres then take the right-hand turn back into the park. This path meanders through the bush for several hundred metres until it reaches the Baumea Bird Hide.

8 At the hide take the left-hand fork in the path, walk for 200 metres and you'll reach Balgay Bird Hide. Another 300 metres on and you are back on the dual use path alongside Jon Saunders Drive, turn right onto it and walk for 60 metres and then take the right-hand fork. The path now continues to meander south between the lake edge and the road, finally staying with the road for 200-300 metres prior to the junction with Herdsman Parade.

9 About 100 metres before you reach this junction, take the path, signposted for the Wildlife Centre, off to the right that immediately skirts a small pond with a large island in the middle of it. Follow this path for approximately 1.6 kilometres back to Selby Street and the Wildlife Centre.

20 Thomsons Lake

Beeliar Regional Park

Thomsons Lake (aka Jilbup Lake) is perhaps one of the most important freshwater lakes on the Swan Coastal Plain. Since the days of first European settlement 75% of the coastal plain has been drained for urban development. Thomsons Lake is a 509-hectare, A-class wetland nature reserve, supporting around 10,000 waterbirds, including more than 1% of the world's population of long toed stints *(Calidris subminuta)*, a small wading bird that migrates from northern Asia to winter in Australia. The park is home to more than 50 species of waterbird, 86 species of "bush bird", 9 species of frogs, 23 species of reptiles, 6 species of mammal and 15 species of ground orchid. Consequently entering into the park is like entering a maximum security prison: it's encircled by 9.2 kilometres of 2-metre high electrified fence!

At a glance

Grade: Medium
Time: 2 hrs
Distance: 6.5 km circuit
Conditions: Best spring to autumn; can flood in winter; lake dries up Jan-Mar
Getting there:
Bus: Nearest bus stop (route 526) is 1 kilometre away
Car: Take the Russell Rd exit off the Kwinana Fwy; car park is on the right after about 2.8 km

This walk ostensibly takes you around the lake's shoreline, but as you walk round you pass through several distinct eco-systems. On the higher ground is the jarrah/banksia woodland of the coastal plain, and there are also zones of flooded gums and swamp paperbarks and, particularly on the eastern side of the lake, a thick belt of rushes and grasses. Tiger snakes are common in wetlands, and areas with an abundance of prey - such as Thomsons Lake - can support large populations. Their venom is very potent and the mortality rate for people who do not receive treatment is over 60%. Thankfully they are shy creatures and it is unlikely you will see one, but it pays to watch where you put your feet when walking through long grass at the lakeside.

20 Thomsons Lake

Walk directions

1 From the car park, enter through the double gate; there is an information board just inside on your right. Walk along the track to the lakeside.

2 At the T-junction turn right (make a mental note of this point so you know where to leave the lakeside at the end of the walk), passing through a gate informing you that you have entered a dieback infected area. Continue around the path to the eastern shore of the lake.

3 During winter and spring this area is prone to flooding - I walked here once in late November and it was knee-deep in places. Using the cover of the reeds it is possible to move closer to the waterbirds on the lake shore and observe them.

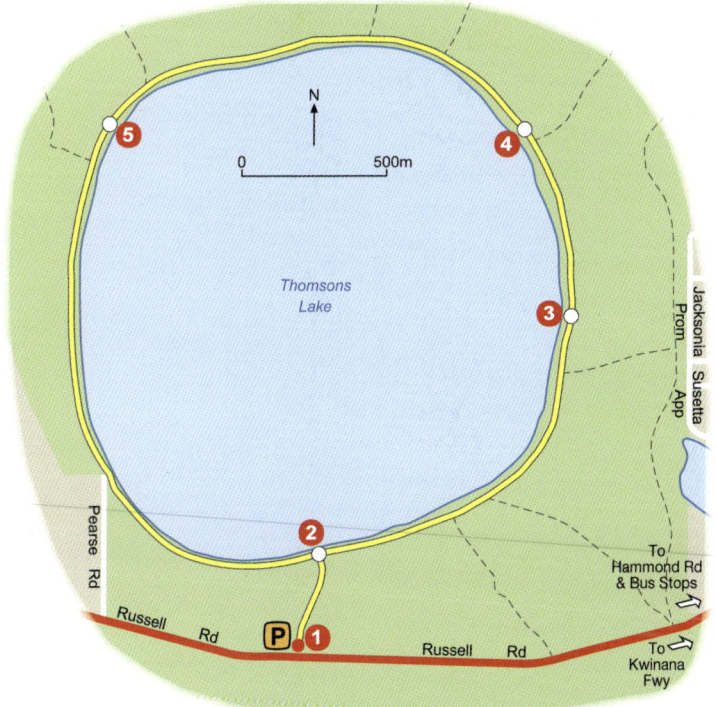

20 Thomsons Lake

4 After a further 500 metres, the path dries out and you return to a mixed woodland of flooded gum and jarrah.

5 You will come to a 4-way junction at the Thomsons Lake Drainage Pumping Station. Go straight ahead. The path now continues along the lake edge until you reach waypoint 2, the point you first walked down to the shore. Turn right here and follow the path back to where you parked your car.

20 Thomsons Lake

21 Yargan's Country

The Spectacles is part of the Beeliar Wetlands and while you will not see the number of birds that you would at the nearby Thompson Lake you will see a very important eco-system: the paperbark swamp, the most extensive in the Beeliar System of Wetlands. The park gives the visitor an idea of what a lot of the Swan Coastal Plain originally looked like. As you walk around this oasis of calm it is hard to believe that you are just a stone's throw away from Western Australia's largest industrial area, Kwinana. The interpretative trail tells of traditional Nyoongar life as told by Joe Walley, a senior traditional custodian and Nyoongar elder. For those who would like to learn more about Nyoongar culture, the local eco-cultural tour, in which Aboriginal people share their knowledge, language and history, is recommended.

At a glance

Grade: Easy
Time: 1 hr 30 mins
Distance: 6 km circuit
Conditions: Not recommended in summer
Getting there:
Car: From the Kwinana Fwy take the Anketell Rd exit; McLaughlin Rd is second on the left; park entrance and parking area are less than a km, on the right
Tours: www.spectaclestours.com.au

21 Yargan's Country

Walk directions

1 From the parking area, walk into the park through the gate and look for the information shelter. Continue on the main path into the park.

2 After 350 metres there is an amphitheater where cultural presentations are given to school groups. Keep walking straight on and you'll come to signs for the *Aboriginal Heritage Walk Trail*, the *Spectacles Walk Trail* and the *Biara Broadwalk* and *Bird Hide*. Veer left to follow the marker for the heritage trail.

3 After 150 metres, the land to your right is covered in a dense woodland of sheoak and river gums with a thick understory of ferns.

A short distance further and you'll reach Burna Kumba ('Big Trees'), which are a marker for the burial site of important members of the Beeliar Midgegooroo.

4 In another 400 metres or so, the area becomes thick with paperbark trees. The paperbark and reeds were used to make bush shelters or Mia Mia.

5 On the most northerly point of the path, the trees thin out and the ground is covered in 'pig face' or bain, a succulent

21 Yargan's Country

which flowers from August to October. The fruit, which are very sweet, can be eaten raw or dried, and early settlers used them to make jam. Nearby are wattle trees, which provide a habitat for the longicorn beetle. The larvae of the beetle are called bardy grubs and Aboriginal people regard them as a bit of a delicacy.

6 When you reach more-or-less the opposite side of the swamp from where you started, you'll see a right-hand turn that takes you into the heart of the paperbark swamp. This swampland is ideal for the long necked turtle or Yargan, one of the Nyoongar totems for the Spectacles. After exploring this side-path, return to the main trail and turn right, continuing your clockwise tour of the swamp.

7 At the end of the *Aboriginal Heritage Walk Trail*, turn right and follow signs for the *Spectacles Walk Trail*. This will lead back to where you started from.

8 It is worth doing the detour to the Biara Boardwalk out to the bird hide to see the swamp paperbark.

21 Yargan's Country

Cottesloe Beach

Coastal Walks

Life's a beach!

If Perth's beaches were anywhere else in the world they would be packed with people and there would be no room to move as there would be deckchairs as far as the eye can see, but thankfully they are not and even at the height of the summer holidays there is plenty of space for everyone. Most Western Australians have a love affair with the coast - the number of people who choose to spend their leisure time fishing, surfing, swimming, sailing, and picnicking is incredible. It's a retiree's dream to use the super cheque to buy a beachside home and it is easy to see why. Quite apart from the natural beauty and the invigorating sea air there is a wonderful laid back beach culture. Precious memories are made up of family trips to the beach, spending the endless summer holidays hanging out with your friends surfing, or dangling a line off a jetty. Walking along the coast is a wonderful way to add to those experiences and further enjoy the beach lifestyle.

22 Guilderton Coastal Walk

At a glance

Grade: Easy to medium
Time: 1 hr 30 mins
Distance: 5 km circuit
Conditions: Good year-round walk; some stretches of beach walking on soft sand

Getting there:

Car: Head north on Waneroo Rd past Yanchep and Two Rocks; soon after Waneroon Rd turns into Lancelin Rd turn left into Guilderton Rd and follow this into town where it turns into Mortimer Rd

Guilderton, on the banks of the Moore River, is a typical sleepy little seaside town north of Perth, more known for its beaches and fishing than anything else. It is also a very pleasant walking destination. The Coastal Walk described here has a bit of everything: beach walking, panoramic 360° views, a lighthouse and the chance to sticky beak some of the delightful vernacular holiday shacks that were once typical of the coastal settlements north of Perth. The corny names of some of the houses are priceless, *That's A Moore Day* and *Forever Moore* are two that readily come to mind. Unfortunately it will not be long before Perth's continual suburban expansion subsumes sleepy Guilderton. There are several other suggested walks on the townsite:

1. Walk across the sandbar at the river mouth to the southern riverbank and the dunes - a 3-kilometre circuit
2. The Lighthouse Loop – a 3-kilometre circuit
3. The Moore River Walk - a 5-kilometre return

The Moore River Walk is particularly fine during spring with the wildflowers of the coastal heathland and the wonderful stands of paper bark trees that have been contorted into weird and wonderful shapes by the strong coastal winds.

22 Guilderton Coastal Walk Pool circuit

Walk directions

1 Start at the car park by the general store and caravan park at the end of Edwards Street. Walk over to the picnic area to the sculpture of the three pelicans and turn right onto the path and follow it around the perimeter of the caravan park, and the cliff base. On your way to Ocean Beach you can see the sandbar that closes off the river mouth to the sea. The bar opens and closes at different times of the year. The path continues along the base of some sand dunes, after a short distance there is a small pathway to your left that takes you down to the beach.

2 Once on the beach follow the shoreline northwards towards the groyne in the distance.

3 After a little over a kilometre you'll reach the groyne - a popular fishing spot. Climb up the steps and turn right following the road up the dune, at the top turn left onto an unsealed road. Shortly after you come to two tracks directly ahead of you: take the right hand one.

4 About 230 metres further on take the left turn up Tank Road towards the lighthouse. After another 280 metres up the dune, turn right and you are at the base of the lighthouse. In 1983, the Federal Department of Transport established a lighthouse at Wreck Point, Guilderton near the river mouth at a cost of $240,000. It was built as an automatic marine beacon and commenced operation in December of that year. It was the only major navigation aid between Fremantle and Jurien Bay, and is also the last to be built in

22 Guilderton Coastal Walk

Western Australia. The new tower, constructed in specially tapered red clay bricks, was 32 metres high and the base was 7.5 metres in diameter. It is possible to walk round the perimeter of the lighthouse, but there is no further public access. Retrace your steps down Tank Road.

5 Just before you get to the turn off that would take you back to the beach, turn left into Forrester Road which at this point is not sealed. After about 300 metres it becomes sealed and shortly after that take the right turn into Gordon Street. After 850 metres you come to a turning on your right which takes you into a car park.

6 Walk across the car park to the pagola at the viewing platform. This has panoramic views of the townsite, the river and ocean beach and is a very pleasant place to sit at the end of a hot summers day to catch the cool breeze off the sea. Walk back across the car park and you'll find a path that takes you down to Ocean Beach again, at the bottom turn left and follow the path back to the general store.

Perth environment - the coastal eco-system

The Perth coastland is largely made up of vegetated sand dunes and, scattered amongst them, limestone outcrops that form cliffs and reefs. The vegetation has stabilized the dunes, preventing them from being eroded by wind and water, and it also protects the limestone which is very fragile and susceptible to chemical and mechanical erosion. This vegetation comprises primarily of sedges, spinifex, wattles, banksias and copses of tuart trees. The beach is the meeting place of the land and marine environment, a place where you see marine crustaceans and molluscs and the birds that feed upon them and the remains of seaweeds that have washed ashore in storms. Offshore are a series of small reefs that run parallel to the coast and provide a rich habitat for an incredible number of marine animals. From the shoreline it is possible to see the top predators of the marine food chain feeding: dolphins, sea lions and sharks.

22 Guilderton Coastal Walk

Perth history – the Vergulde Draeck

In 1931, forty 17th century silver guilder were coins found in the sand hills near the entrance to the Moore River. They were believed to be from the wreck of the Dutch ship, the Vergulde Draeck ("Guilded Dragon") that had foundered on a reef just north of Moore River near Ledge Point in 1656. The wreck of the ship, which had been carrying a valuable cargo, including silver coins worth 185,000 guilders, was not discovered until 1963.

23 Mindarie Dunes Walk

When I think of sand dunes my mind immediately conjures up visions of the Sahara Desert with Gary Cooper playing Beau Geste lost in an inhospitable wasteland. The dunes at Mindarie are part of the Quindalup dune system, a system of vegetated coastal dunes and a prominent feature of the coastal plain that the Perth Metro is situated on. These dunes once supported a wide variety of flora and fauna and were a very important ecosystem. Most of the housing in Perth's northern suburbs is built on these dunes, but thankfully some small pockets remain and this is one of them. When you are done walking you might wish to retire to the nearby Indian Ocean Brewing Company for suitable refreshment...

At a glance

Grade: Medium
Time: 1 hr 30 mins
Distance: 4 km one way
Conditions: Beach walking on soft sand; Spring and early summer best to see the wildflowers

Getting there:
Bus: 482 from Clarkson rail station stops on Anchorage Dr
Car: Parking on Long Beach Prom, off Anchorage Dr

Further Information:
www.wanneroo.wa.gov.au

23 Mindarie Dunes Walk

Walk directions

1 It is no longer possible to drive into the reserve so park in the bays provided on Long Beach Promenade. Walk through the gates and down the asphalt path, after 125 metres it changes to compressed limestone rubble. At the junction turn left.

2 After about 150 metres you'll be walking in a 'hollow' formed by two dunes. These hollows create a more hospitable microclimate that allows the growth of flora not normally associated with a beach environment, such as the Tuart trees you can see here. This is nearly the northernmost limit for Tuart trees and they are usually quite stunted in the warmer and drier climate, but here they are growing to near normal size. Despite the shelter provided by the dunes you can see from the way the trees are bent over that they are subjected to very strong winds coming in from the sea. As you climb the next dune the path surface turns to loose sand and remains so for most of the remainder of the walk. At the top are two wooden barriers - walk round them as they are there to deter dirt bike riders. Take the next left, and the area you are now walking through is very typical of the coastal heathland with sedges, spinefex, wattles and dryandras.

3 Take the next right turn and climb the steep dune. At the top you are rewarded with your first glimpse of the sea.

4 At the next junction turn left. As you walk through the dunes you can tantalizingly hear the sound of the surf on the beach, yet it seems like you are never getting any closer. At the present you are in fact walking parallel to the beach. Please avoid the temptation to short cut as this damages the sparse vegetation and leads to erosion.

23 Mindarie Dunes Walk

5 Cross straight over at the next intersection and continue for another 200 metres before turning sharp right onto the beach. In the distance is Mindarie Groyne: walk towards that.

6 The beach by the groyne is a popular surfing spot for the local kids and you can usually see some of them no matter what the weather is doing. Climb up the wooden steps near the end of the beach and then turn right and walk through the car park, through the gate at its far end and on to a track. Keep left until you come out on Long Beach Promenade, near the junction with Anchorage Drive. Turn right and follow the pavement back to where you left your car.

24 Trigg Mountain

"Trigg Mountain" is the local name for the Trigg Bushland Reserve, considered one of the most important nature reserves in Perth. It is one of the state government's 'Bush Forever' sites and is a designated reference site for the Perth Region Plant Biodiversity Project. The reserve is on a series of parabolic sand dunes that have been stabilized by vegetation over the last 6,000 years. This walk trail takes you through the upper reaches of the reserve where you'll see that the native flora is quite different to that down on the coast. You can expect to see the cushion fan flower *(Scaevola crassifolia)* and the coast daisy-bush *(Olearia axillarius)*, which is very easy to spot with its characteristic blue-grey leaves. This is also one of the last places in Perth to see naturally occurring groves of Rottnest Cypress *(Callitris preissii)* which before European settlement was very common. Summer scented wattle *(Acacia rostelliferra)* and tuart trees *(Eucalyptus gomphocephala)* are also found on the slopes behind the school. Corkybark *(Gyrostemon ramulosus)* can also be found which is unusual as it is rarely seen this far southwest as it prefers a hotter drier climate. (The Friends of Trigg Bushland have put out a very comprehensive checklist for the flora found in the reserve.) In terms of wildlife the native large mammals have long gone, but 65 species of birds have been recorded with notable highlights including ring-necked parrots, red wattle birds, pardalotes and the white-browed scrubwren.

At a glance

Grade: Easy
Time: 1 hr 15 mins
Distance: 4.3 km circuit
Conditions: Best in spring and early summer for wildflowers; one long section of steps
Getting there:
Bus: 423 stops on Karrinyup Rd, just after West Coast Hwy (then a 700-metre walk)
Car: Park at Kevan Langdon Res, on Elliot Rd, just off West Coast Hwy
Dogs: Yes
Further Information:
Friends Of Trigg Bushland, www.triggbushland.org.au

24 Trigg Mountain

Walk directions

1 Park on the school side of the car park in Kevan Langdon Reserve, then walk through Milligan Reserve keeping the school on your left-hand side.

2 When you come to a gate, go through and continue straight on. After about another 170 metres, turn left at the T-junction.

3 At the next junction, in about 200 metres, turn right and carry on up the dune. On your right you will pass a grove of Rottnest cypress, and a bit further up on your left is the ubiquitous parrot bush and some coastal daisy-bush.

4 Turn left at the next junction and after 120 metres you will crest the dune and see the sea. To your left you can see Observation City at Scarborough, and on the horizon is Rottnest Island. As you walk along the top of the dune you can see dune sheoaks on either side of the path. When you come to a crossroads turn left.

5 At the school boundary fence turn sharp right, and follow the path as it runs parallel to Karrinyup Road and adjacent to the school. After the path veers around

24 Trigg Mountain

to the left, go down the steps and turn left at the bottom. Walk past the school entrance and, just after, cross the road and go through the turnstile. The path angles back to your right, runs parallel to Elliot Road for a short way and then veers around to the left to run parallel with the West Coast Highway.

6 Ignore the left turn at the next junction and carry straight on up the dune. When you get to the top you will be able to see the sea again and on a warm day you get the benefit of the cooling sea breeze. Turn left at the next T-junction, and veer left again at the next junction.

7 Turn right at the next T-junction to bring you back to Elliott Road. Walk through the turnstile, cross the road and you are back in the Kevan Langdon Reserve. It is now just a short walk back to the start point.

24 Trigg Mountain

Perth culture - Wardarn (Ocean) Dreaming

A long time ago, back in the dreamtime some spirit children were trapped by the rising sea, so to save themselves they attached themselves to young whales (mimang) and dolphins (kila). Now whenever a whale or dolphin beaches itself the Nyoongar believe that is one of the spirit children returning home. The coast is a special place for the Nyoongar because when a clan member died they were either buried on a dreaming trail or in the sand of the nearest coastal dunes. Djenark - the silver gull - flies over the coast and the land maintaining the links between those Nyoongar buried inland and those buried on the coast.

25 Cottesloe Beach Walk

Think beach, think Norfolk Pines... you must be thinking about Cottesloe. Internationally famous for its beach, laid back lifestyle and marvelous Indian Ocean sunsets.

The first European visitors were the Dutch in 1697 when Willem de Vlamingh and his three ships made a brief stop over. They were looking for the ship and crew of a Dutch East Indies ship and in the process discovered the southwest of Western Australia and called it New Holland. They were here for just about a week and in that time they had a bit of an explore. The French were the next visitors in 1801 and in 1829 the British arrived, but it was not until 1886 that the district was named Cottesloe. Soon after, with sea breezes being considered good for the constitution, Cottesloe began to attract tourists and the beach life was born. Over the intervening years between then and now Cottesloe has become synonymous with a relaxed beach lifestyle and walking along the beachfront is a fantastic way to enjoy it.

At a glance

Grade: Easy
Time: 1 hr
Distance: 4 km one way
Conditions: Good year-round walk; pushchair friendly
Getting there:
Bus: Regular service along Marine Pde
Train: Grant St rail station
Car: Parking on the corner of Marine Pde and Grant St, Cottesloe, by Grant Marine Park
Further Information: www.cottesloe.wa.gov.au

25 Cottesloe Beach Walk

Walk directions

1 Start at Grant Marine Park, then cross Marine Parade and head southwards along the dual use path.

2 Cottesloe Beach is a Perth institution, so popular and attracting so many people in summer that you can almost smell the sunscreen from Marine Parade! There are grommets boogie boarding, young guys playing beach volleyball and looking to impress, and the beautiful people are there just to hang out and be seen. The Indiana Tearooms, looking like the offspring of Moghul and Federation architecture, overlooks the beach and is perfectly positioned to afford views of simply stunning sunsets while its patrons enjoy dinner. Just next door to the tearooms is French

Landing, a memorial to the French survey ship that ran aground here in 1801. During their enforced stay some of the crew went south to the mouth of the Swan River at Fremantle and planted the French Tricolor to signal to the other ships in the fleet. Another group sailed down the Swan as far as the mouth of the Canning River. The memorial was set up to celebrate the bicentenary of the visit in 2001.

3 Nearly opposite Jarrad Street, the Cottesloe Sundial was built for the Australian Bicentennial celebrations. It is modeled upon sundials in India built by the Maharajah Jai Singh in the 18th century (Jantar Mantar can be seen in Delhi were it attracts hundreds of thousands of visitors).

25 Cottesloe Beach Walk

4 A little further along and you'll be walking alongside the Cottesloe Reef Fish Habitation Area which lies just offshore. This amazingly diverse underwater habitat and the fish communities that it supports are within easy reach of the beach here and consequently the reef is a popular snorkeling and scuba diving spot.

5 The end of this walk is heralded by the Vlamingh Memorial, supposedly where the Dutch landed in 1697. There are good views both northwards and southwards along the coast from the platform and the beach here is a dog beach, so if you have brought your faithful companion you can let them discharge some energy with a runaround. To get back to the start you can either the walk back the way you came, or walked to the Victoria Street station and catch the train back to Grant Street. Between the station and the park is Daisies Deli on the corner of Grant and Marmion Streets - their muffins are the best in Western Australia!

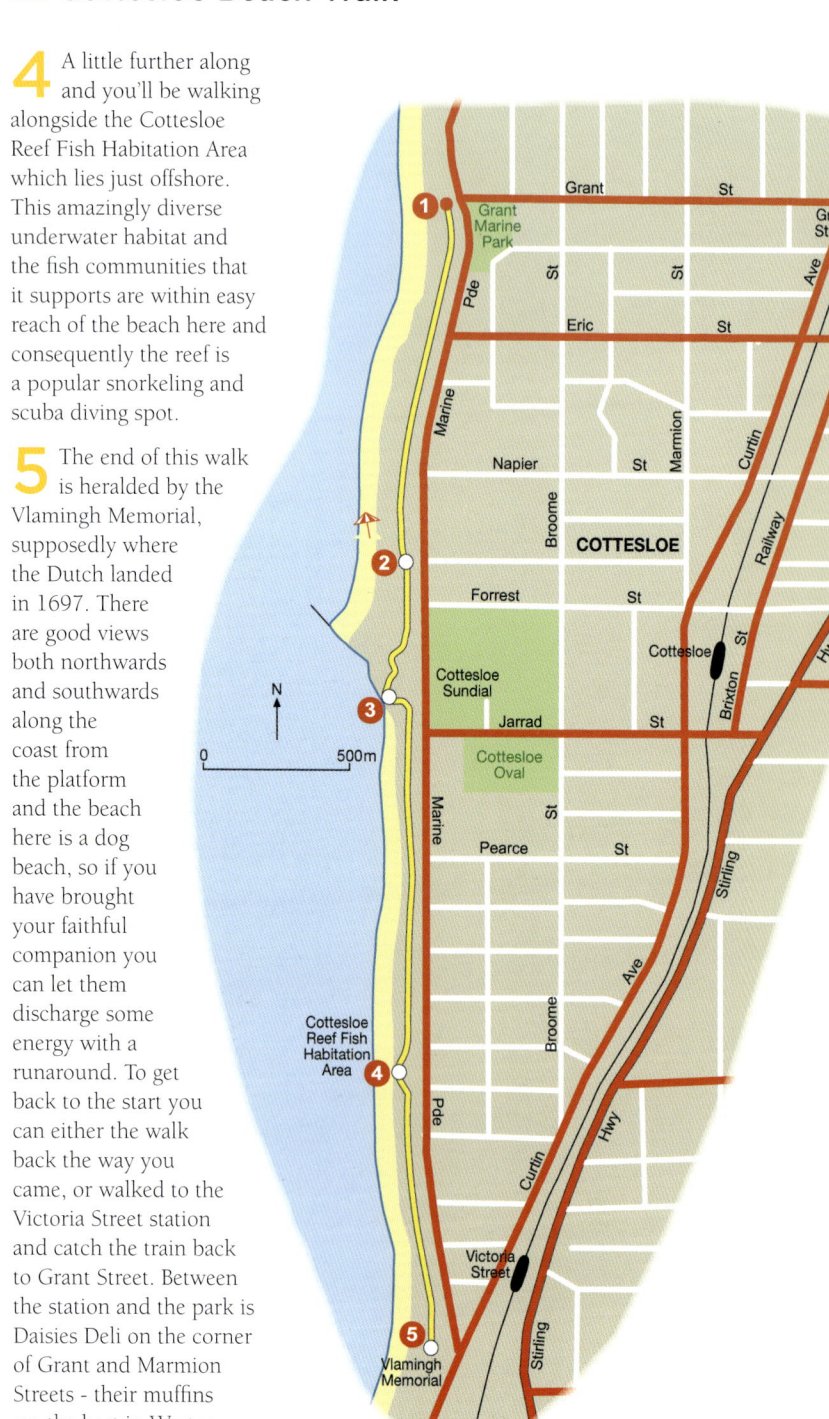

25 Cottesloe Beach Walk

26 Woodman Point Walk

Woodman Point is used primarily for recreation, the John Graham Reserve (the starting point for the walk) having extensive recreational facilities. Most of these are floodlit, making it a great place for a family picnic on a summer's evening. There is a jetty at the reserve and it and the rocks at the headland are both popular fishing and diving spots. There is also a nature reserve, home to the most extensive stand of Rottnest Pine *(Callitris preissii)* on the mainland, plus seventy other species of native plant and a large number of migratory wading birds, which should keep budding naturalists happy for hours. When I was last there I inadvertently interrupted a wedged tailed eagle *(Aquila audax)* taking a crested tern *(Santalum acuminatum)* while walking along the path.

At a glance

Grade: Easy
Time: 1 hr 45 mins
Distance: 7 km circuit
Conditions: Year-round walk; pushchair friendly
Getting there:
Bus: Bus services stop in Cockburn Rd
Car: Car park at the end of Nyyerbup Cir, off Cockburn Rd, south of Fremantle

26 Woodman Point Walk

Walk directions

1 From the car park in the John Graham Reserve, follow the path through the picnic area and down to the jetty where pelicans can often be seen sitting on the jetty lamp posts.

2 Just before the jetty is a path off to the left, and as you walk along it you will see a fenced off nature reserve on your left. Shortly after the path does a bit of a dogleg to the right – continue following the path, ignoring all left and right side-tracks, towards the Cockburn Cement Jetty in the far distance.

3 After nearly 2 kilometres the path bends round 90° to the left. Carry straight on through the trees for a very short way to come alongside Woodman Point View Road. Cross over and follow the road to your right until, after about 200 metres, you come to a car park on your left.

Take the path that veers off to the left at the far end of the car park, then follow this as it parallels the foreshore until you reach the breakwater.

4 After taking in the views, retrace your steps to waypoint 3, but then carry straight on along the path between the road and the shore. After about 600 metres the path makes a firm departure from the road and continues on for about 300 metres, coming out on a road (Jervoise Bay Cove).

5 Directly over the road, opposite is a dual use path. Take this, following the signs for the Beach/BBQ Area. After crossing another road (O'Kane Court) you'll pass through

a stand of large Tuart Trees (*Eucalyptus gomphocephala*).

6 The path crosses a couple of other paths and after 300 metres there's a fork. The main path

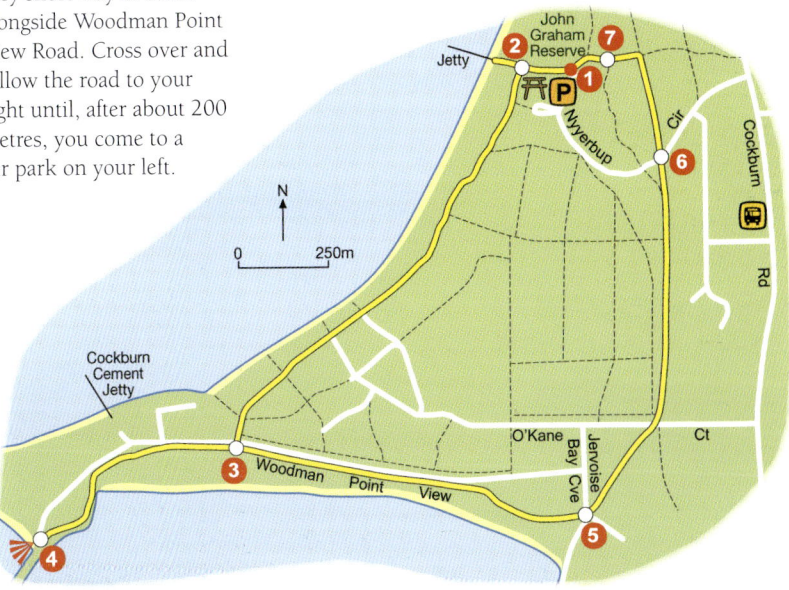

26 Woodman Point Walk

veers away to the left, but carry straight on to cross another road (Nyyerbup Circuit) where you'll find Quandong Trees (*Santalum acuminatum*) on either side of the path. These are a hemi-parasitic plant which use the root systems of other plants for nutrients and are in the sandalwood family. The fruit was used by the Nyoongars as a bush food and bush medicine and the wood from the trees had a very high oil content making it very flammable, so it was used as a friction stick to light fires. Early settlers used the fruit to make jams and chutneys, and this tradition continues today. Now the fruit is in demand overseas and the trees are cultivated commercially.

7 At the next path junction turn left. After about 100 metres you'll be in the picnic and BBQ area of the John Graham Reserve and at the northern end of the car park where you started.

Perth history – Woodman Point

Woodman Point was first set aside as a quarantine station for livestock in the 19th century. In 1904 part of the station was given over to quarantine migrants and it saw heavy use during the Spanish Flu Pandemic after the First World War. It also saw service as an internment camp during the Second World War and was used as an explosive dump concurrently until the mid-1980s. The Commonwealth Government officially closed it as a quarantine station in 1979. Many of the buildings, including the dormitories are now used for school and other groups and the complex is known as Woodman Point Recreation Camp. So it would be fair to say that Woodman Point has had a varied and interesting history.

26 Woodman Point Walk

27 Cape Peron

Cape Peron (also known as Point Peron), in the Rockingham Lakes Regional Park, is a headland located at the extreme southern end of Cockburn Sound and forms the northern boundary of the Shoalwater Marine Park. The cape is named after the French naturalist François Peron who accompanied Baudin on his epic voyage of discovery around Australia in 1801. The cape has rugged limestone cliffs, reefs and beautiful panoramic views. The cliffs and rock formations are, in geological terms, a very dynamic and constantly evolving landscape as they are easily eroded by wind, water, and sand. Caves and overhangs form where waves have undercut the cliff faces and eventually they collapse. The limestone is, as you will see, very fragile and unstable and there are warning signs highlighting the risks - please take note of them. As you walk this trail you will discover the remnants of one of the Second World War coastal batteries that were built to defend the approach to Garden Island and Fremantle. There is also an observation post on the highest point of the cape, which has views out over Cockburn Sound, Garden Island, Penguin Island and Seal Island. If you face east on a clear day you can just about make out the Darling Scarp. In summer remember to bring your bathers as you can finish the walk with a dip in Mangles Bay.

At a glance
Grade: Easy
Time: 1 hr
Distance: 2.7 km circuit
Conditions: Year-round walk
Getting there:
Bus: Nearest stop (the 551) is on the corner of Safety Bay Rd and Parkin St (2.6 kms)
Car: Mangles Bay car park is at the end of Point Peron Rd in Rockingham

27 Cape Peron

Walk directions

1 Around the far edge of the Mangles Bay car park is a pavement. Take the path just off it that heads up the hill, veering first towards the right and shortly back around to the left.

2 At the top of the hill is the WWII observation post. There are some steep steps back down to the car park, useful if you have boisterous children and you want to tire them out, but the path you want is on the far side of the lookout.

3 When you reach the junction, after about 150 metres, take the right turn (the left turn takes you to the Shoalwater Bay car park and straight on leads to a small beach). You'll soon pass the ruins of gun emplacements on your right - the guns have long gone and all that remains are a few concrete structures. Continue along the cliff-top path, keeping left at a junction.

4 Take the left turn at the next T-junction and head downhill back toward the shore. Ignore the first track heading off to the left (down to the beach) but take the second. This short stretch loops closer to the shore before emerging back on the main track – when it does, turn left.

5 Turn left at the next junction and walk to the lookout. Retrace your steps a short way and follow the track just above the shoreline around to the rock platform of Cape Peron.

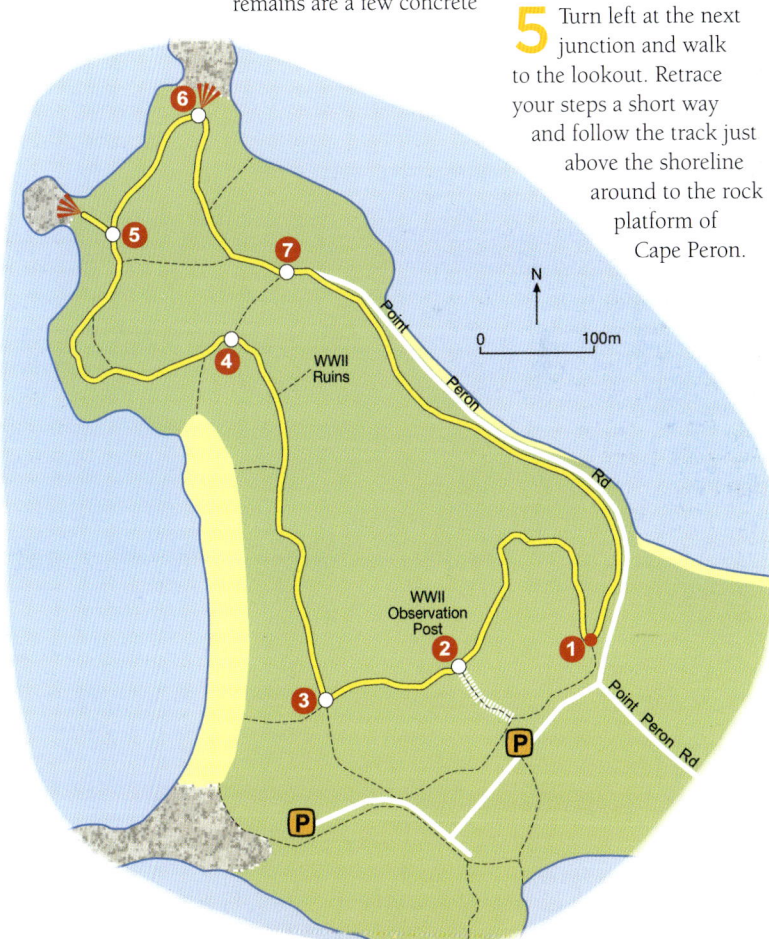

27 Cape Peron

From here you can see the whole 4-kilometre length of the causeway that links Garden Island to the mainland.

6 You'll see another, larger track heading back up from the cape. Take this as it curves around to the left. Ignore the two side-tracks that head off to the left and then to the right.

7 Take the next left-hand turnoff signposted for John's Point. There is a very nice beach here. Carry on following the signs back to Mangle Beach and then follow the path back to the car park where you started.

27 Cape Peron

28 Rockingham Waterfront Walk

Rockingham is named after a ship that brought settlers to Western Australia in 1830. The ship ran aground and was repaired but never regained seaworthiness and was left to sink in Careening Bay. The town was eventually gazetted in 1897. Today Rockingham has some of the finest coastline and parks in the Perth Metro area. There is a thriving eco tourism industry based upon the local wildlife with dolphin, penguin and seal cruises that visit the various small islands in the Shoalwater Islands Marine Park. This walk traces part of the coastline of Mangles Bay and on one level it lets visitors enjoy in invigorating experience of walking along the beachfront and enjoying a day at the seaside, while on another deeper level the walk lets visitors explore the Rockingham community's connection with their past and the relationship with the sea through a series of public art works.

At a glance

Grade: Easy
Time: 1 hr 45 mins
Distance: 5.6 km return
Conditions: Not a winter walk; pushchair friendly
Getting there:
Bus/Train: 555 Shuttle Bus from Rockingham station to Railway Terr, buses also run along Kent St
Car: Park near the corner of Alexandra St and Rockingham Beach Rd
Dogs: On a lead only and not on the beach.
Further Information:
www.rockingham-tourism.com

28 Rockingham Waterfront Walk

Walk directions

1 The start point is Alexandra Reserve, at the end of Alexandra Street, where you'll find toilets and BBQ facilities. Standing on the path that runs along the beachfront, you are looking out over Mangles Bay. Northeast up the coast is the Kwinana industrial area, and in front of you is Garden Island, a Royal Australian Navy base which is connected to the mainland via a 4-kilometre causeway. Turn to your left - as you walk along this path you are following the Waterfront Pioneer Rotary Public Art Work. There are brass plaques set into the path that commemorate key events, places and people in Rockingham's history.

2 Continue past the beachfront cafés and restaurants.

3 The large sculpture of flying geese at Palm Beach is the Catalpa Memorial by artists Charlie Smith and Joan Walsh

Smith. The wild goose in Irish mythology represents freedom and the sculpture represents the flight from repression. In 1868 a number of Irish Fenians were sent to Western Australia as convicts, and a year later one of them, John O'Reilly, with help from the locals, escaped from the penal colony and went to America. In 1876 O'Reilly returned on the US whaling ship Catalpa and enabled the remaining Fenian prisoners to escape.

28 Rockingham Waterfront Walk

4 A little further along, the Palm Beach jetty was originally built for the navy during the Second World War. Just in front of it is the memorial to Z Force, the special forces unit that operated behind Japanese lines in South-East Asia. They trained in small one and four man submarines in Cockburn Sound. An account of their activities is given in Jack Wong Sue's book *Blood On Borneo*.

5 Continue walking and a little further on from the jetty on the other side of the Esplanade is the Rotary Park. This lake with its waterfall and trees is a waterbird reserve and there is an information board telling you what bird species can be seen there. Retrace your steps back to the jetty opposite the Cruising Yacht Club, cross the Esplanade and turn right into Railway Terrace, then turn left into Kent street.

6 As you walk along Kent Street you pass the Tourist Information Center, and just past that is the Rockingham Museum in the old Roads Board Office (see www.rockingham-tourist.com/1/museum). Next door is the Rockingham arts and Craft Centre, with a gift shop selling locally produced items and, on the first floor, a gallery.

7 On the corner of Kent and Wanliss Streets is Derbal Nara Community Garden. The landscaping of the park tells of the dreamtime story of the crocodile and the creation of Garden Island. Local community artists and students from local schools have created totem poles and mosaics. Turn left into Wanliss Street and walk to the intersection with Rockingham Beach road. Cross over, turn right and walk back to Alexandra Reserve.

29 Penguin Island

Penguin Island is a tiny 12.5-hectare island, 700 metres off the coast at Rockingham in the Shoalwater Islands Marine Park. It might strike some people as an odd place to go for a walk, but it is truly well worth the effort if you have any interest in nature. The island is home to Western Australia's largest colony of little penguins *(Eudyptula minor)* and is also one of only nine breeding sites for the Australian pelican *(Pelicanus conspicillatus)* in Australia. Numerous other bird species can also be seen readily on the island and include giant petrels, oyster catchers, pied cormorants and several different types of terns. The waters surrounding Penguin Island provide a habitat for bottlenose dolphins, Australian sea lions and marine turtles.

At a glance
Grade: Easy
Time: 1 hr
Distance: 1.6 km circuit
Conditions: Island open mid-Sept to early June; at time of writing not suitable for pushchairs, but the broadwalk is being upgraded with completion due Nov 2010
Getting there:
Bus: The 552 and 553 from Rockingham station stop on Penguin Rd, 900 metres from the ferry jetty
Car: Parking near Mersey Point Jetty, Arcadia Dr, Shoalwater
Further Information: www.penguinisland.com.au

The best way to enjoy the island is to make a day of it, catch the feeding time at the Penguin Experience Centre, then take the glass bottomed boat to Seal Island and finally do the walk on your return to Penguin Island. If you still have energy to spare after all that then there is also the North Penguin Island Snorkel Trail as well. There are no facilities on the island other than the provision of drinking water and toilets so bring everything you think you might need with you. People do walk across the sandbar to Penguin Island but the Department of Environment and Conservation do not recommend it. Strong rips and currents in the bay and potholes in the sandbar have caused people to drown while attempting the crossing.

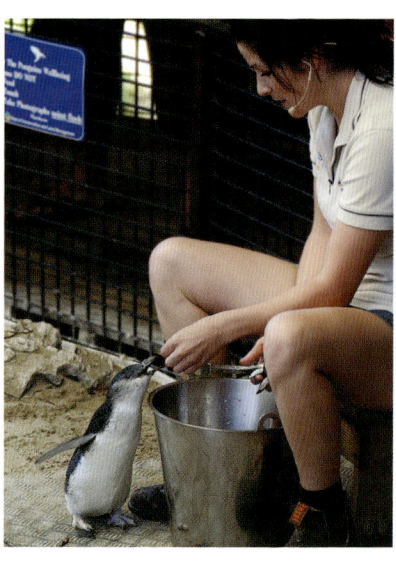

29 Penguin Island

Walk directions

1 Walk up the jetty from where you disembarked the ferry and head towards the Penguin Experience Centre. There is a very comprehensive information board that details the islands eco-system, it's history and the flora and fauna living there.

2 In front of the centre is a shaded picnic spot, with drinking water and toilets. Follow the broadwalk round to the right past the toilets towards the northern lookout.

3 After 230 metres there is a turn off on your right that goes down to the beach, passing McKenzie's Well. Once on the beach you pass a series of caves in the limestone cliffs. Seaforth McKenzie enlarged several of the caves and used them to provide services for the visitors to the island. One was a library and one was a store. If you look carefully at the limestone you can clearly see the fossilized remains of plants, which show that the surrounding area was once on the seabed. Return to the broadwalk and turn right.

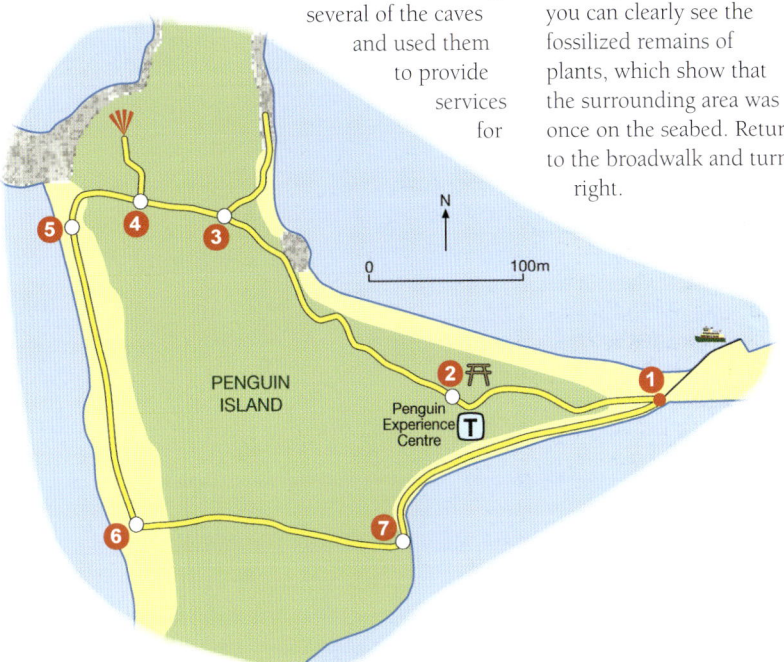

29 Penguin Island

4 After a little over 50 metres, turn right at another junction and walk up to the northern lookout. From here you can see the pelican nesting site, and past that Shag Island, Seal Island and Point Peron on the mainland. Retrace your steps to rejoin the main trail, turn right and follow it down onto the beach.

5 On the beach turn left and follow the shoreline. This is the 'weather' side of the island where the ocean and wind hit the shore with their full force. There is a limestone wave cut platform, and the cliffs at the far end of the beach show evidence of being undercut by waves.

6 After 200 metres of beach walking there is a sign pointing at a gap in the dunes on your left. It is a bit of a slog to climb

the sand dunes, but come November 2010 it should be replace by a broadwalk.

7 Once over the dunes and down the other side you'll emerge onto another beach. Turn left and you will soon come out out behind the Penguin Experience Centre. Carry on walking straight down the beach to get back to the ferry jetty.

29 Penguin Island

Little penguin *(Eudyptula minor)*

Perth personalities - Seaforth McKenzie

There is only one way to describe this man and that is as one of life's true eccentrics. The Canadian born New Zealander started living on the island in 1914. In 1918 he leased it with the intention of developing a tourist resort, and he had himself crowned "King of Penguin Island" in a grandiose ceremony in the Palace Cave. In 1926 McKenzie left the island and went home to New Zealand to his wife and six children after an absence of forty five years. His excuse was that he left for work one day as usual but lost his memory, and upon regaining it he went home.

The Darling Range

The Darling Range is a series of hills running behind a low escarpment that stretches from north of Bindoon to south of Pemberton, and eastwards to include Mount Bakewell in York and Mount Saddleback near Boddington. This is a biologically diverse environment with an impressive range of native flora and fauna, much of which can be seen nowhere else in the world.

The Western Australian Government has created a network of thirteen national parks in the Perth Hills district for conservation and recreation. Add to this four regional parks at Chidlow, Kalamunda, Kelmscott and Wungong, plus thousands of hectares of state forest, and it's easy to see the tremendous potential for recreational activities. The Perth Hills draw hundreds of thousands of visitors each year, between them enjoying picnic sites, mountain biking, horse riding, canoeing and white water rafting as well as bushwalking.

Note: at the time of writing there is a parliamentary inquiry considering the 2007 proposal from the Department of Water to ban activities including bushwalking within water catchment areas. A good many of the traditional bushwalking areas close to Perth lie within a catchment, so if you are considering one of these walks double-check that access is still permissible.

30 The Echidna Trail

Walyunga National Park straddles the Swan Valley. The woodland is largely composed of wandoo (Eucalyptus wandoo) on the valley sides, marri (Corymbia calophylla) and powder bark (Eucalyptus accedens) on the ridge tops and flooded gums (Eucalyptus rudis) and paperbark trees (Melaleuca rhaphiophylla) on the river bank. The park is home to a huge variety of other plants including Zamia Palms (Macrozamia fraseri), grass trees (Xanthorrhoea preisii), dryandras, grevilleas and twelve orchid species. Despite the park being surrounded by farmland and housing developments, many native animals live within it. The resident kookaburras are not adverse to stealing sausages from the BBQs. Up until late in the last century the valley contained one of the largest Nyoongar campsites and the main tribal group was the Whadjuck. The coastal tribes would come up to Walyunga to trade with the hill tribes. There is some uncertainty as to the meaning of Walyunga; some believe that it means "northern Nyoongar" while others believe it roughly translates as "happy place".

There are several walking trails within the park, all of which are well-sign posted and easy to follow. The Echidna Trail was partially funded by the Rotary Club so as to allow walkers the opportunity to enjoy a wide variety of wildflowers in a varied landscape.

At a glance

Grade: Medium to hard
Time: 4 hrs
Distance: 10.5 km circuit
Ascent/descent: 244 m ascent/descent
Conditions: Well-signposted route on gravel tracks with some very steep descents on unsteady surfaces; avoid in summer
Getting there:
Car: Travel up the Great Northern Highway, turn right just before Bulls-brook onto Walyunga Road – the walk begins closest to the first car park, at Walyunga Pool (note that the nearest bus stop is over 5 km away)
Further Information: www.naturebase.net, T 9571 1371

32 The Echidna Trail

Walk directions

1 At the far end of the Walyunga Pool picnic area is a sign detailing all the walks; this is the starting point. Initially the Echidna Trail follows the same route as the Kangaroo Trail so follow its markers. Cross the road and go up the steps, turning left away from the ranger's residence. Past the park entry booth is Dicky Jones' Creek, named after a ticket-of-leave convict who lived nearby with his Nyoongar wife.

2 At this point the trail divides – there is an information board with a map detailing the various options. Carry straight on along the Echidna Trail. After 2 kilometres take the

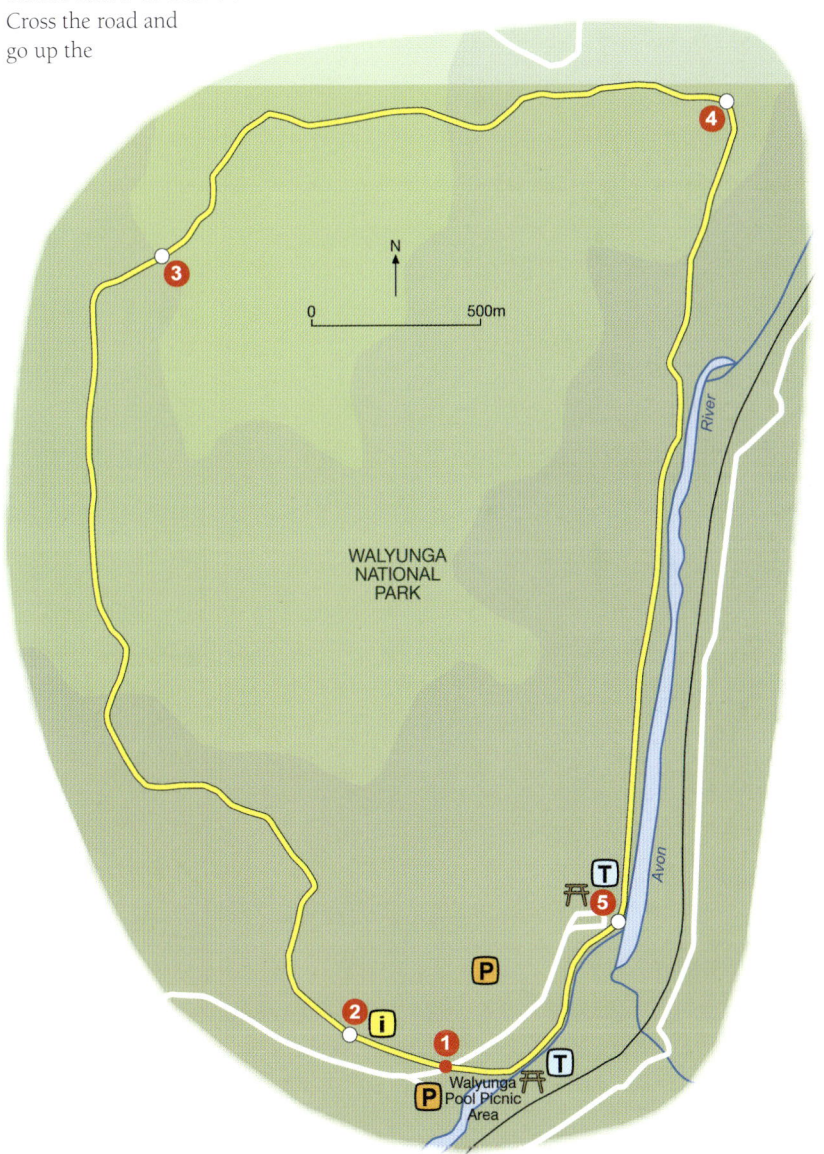

32 The Echidna Trail

turn off to the right and start climbing up the valley side. The woodland opens up and at the top of a steep climb there is a lookout offering views over the Swan Valley. Once you reach the ridge top you will have views out across the Swan Coastal Plain.

3 Here the Echidna Trail joins with the Kingfisher Trail. If you are feeling foot-sore and weary the quickest way back to the car park is to follow the Kingfisher Trail. Back on the Echidna trail the path turns right at Dicky Jones' Gully. A short, steep climb takes you to the summit of Woodsome Hill, which at 260 metres elevation is the highest point in the park and has a fire tower at its peak. This area was first surveyed in 1854 and was part of the Woodsome Estate that covered 16,200 hectares of the Swan Valley. This is also the halfway point, and the rocks at the base of the tower make a good place to take a break.

4 Climbing steeply down the slope you will find a lookout over the Swan Valley. On the opposite side you can see a red dirt road; just underneath it is the railway line that links Perth with the rest of Australia via Kalgoorlie. This line opened in 1966 and replaced the old Mahogany Creek Diversion (see the John Forest Heritage Trail for more details). At the 6 kilometre mark turn right and carry on heading down towards the river. Take care – this section is very steep and has a treacherous gravel surface. After a long descent take the right-hand track towards the riverbank. It is here that the trail becomes Syd's Rapids Trail. The rapids – a popular canoeing spot and part of the Avon Descent white water race – are named after Syd Ambler, one of the first canoeists to shoot the Walyunga Rapids. Flooded river gums inhabit the river bank area and are easy to identify with their grey flaky lower bark and their smooth grey upper bark.

5 The trail now joins the Aboriginal Heritage Trail, this interpretive walk explores the significance of Walyunga to the Nyoongar people. Keep your eyes open for long neck turtles as in spring they leave the river and climb the banks to lay their eggs. In summer the new hatchlings can be seen scurrying to the safety of the water. Eventually you will be led back to waypoint 1 at the Walyunga Pool picnic area.

32 The Echidna Trail

31 John Forrest Heritage Trail

Following the route of the Eastern Railway through the Jane Brook Valley, the John Forrest Heritage road is only a small part of the Railways Heritage Trail, a walking and cycling trail that runs along a disused railway reserve between Midland and Wooroloo. In the 1870s timber companies built their own railway lines to transport timber to Fremantle prior to being exported. In the 1880s the Western Australian government realised the need for a rail network that would link the state with the rest of Australia. Work commenced on the Mahogany Creek Deviation in 1894 and the first trains started to use the line in 1896. The new railway raised public awareness of how attractive the Jane Brook Valley was and in 1898 an area of land was set aside for preservation. In 1900 that reserve had the distinction of being declared the second national park in Australia. In 1947 the park was renamed after the explorer and the state's first premier Sir John Forrest. The railway line remained in use until 1966 when it was replaced by the current route through the Avon Valley.

At a glance

Grade: Medium
Time: 2.5 hrs
Distance: 10 km one way (12 km if you explore the waterfalls and rock garden)
Conditions: Aug-Dec is peak time for waterfalls and wildflowers
Getting there:
Bus: The 323 bus from Midland Rail Station stops at Viveash Rd, just before Tunnel Rd (stop number 15286) and it's a 900 m walk from there to the start of the trail

Car: Turn left off the Great Eastern Hwy onto the Old York Rd, left onto Swan View Rd, left onto Curve Rd then right onto Pechey Rd

Further Information: www.dec.wa.gov.au, T 9298 8344 (for info on the history of the trail, see www.mundaringtourism.com.au/walk-and-cycle.html)

31 John Forrest Heritage Trail

Walk directions

1 Begin at the car park off Pechey Road. Walk through the white gate and follow the wide trail to where signs mark the commencement of the trail.

2 Veer right towards the western entrance to the Swan View Tunnel, the only railway tunnel in Western Australia. Work began in 1894 and it presented quite a challenge as the granite rock was unstable. The resulting 340 metre long tunnel had to have masonry walls and an arched brick ceiling to prevent rock falls. In all the tunnel was completed in twelve months at a cost of £12,160 10s 7d. Eventually you will pass the eastern tunnel entrance – carry straight on.

3 At this point you will have the opportunity to visit the National Park Waterfalls – these drop 25 metres and the water runs after the first winter rains until December. In the right season a quick trip to the falls can be worth a look. Once you've had your fill return to waypoint 3 and carry on along the trail.

4 Not far from the falls is the National Park Rail Station – this was built in 1936 to allow day trippers from Perth to travel by rail to the park. Previously tourists had to disembark at Hovea Station and then walk the 1.7 kilometres to the picnic area. Continue along the track towards the Jane Brook.

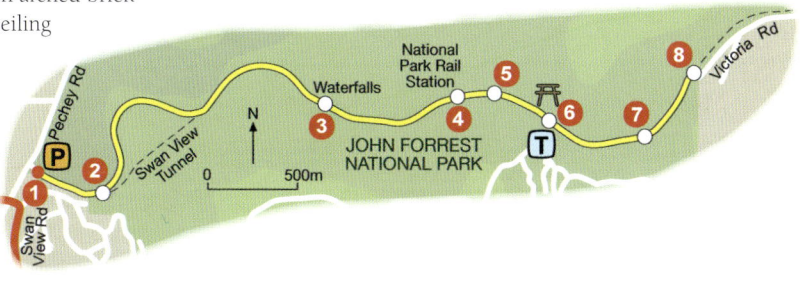

31 John Forrest Heritage Trail

5 The Jane Brook Bridge was built in 1895 from locally cut jarrah. However, it became apparent that it was not suited to carrying the loads that were using the line and it was shaking and swaying as the trains crossed. In 1928 the timber bridge was replaced with the current steel and concrete structure.

6 A short distance from the bridge are the Rock Gardens and tearooms, built in the 1930s by over 400 sustenance workers made unemployed during the Great Depression. Similar projects took place at Araluen and Yanchep. Here there are also toilets and picnic and barbecue facilities.

7 After crossing over Jane Brook, the next stop along the track is the Hovea Falls – named after the holly-leaved Hovea that grows in the area.

8 Last stop just along from the falls is the Hovea Station, once used by locals commuting to work in Midland. Sadly the palm trees, the foundations of the station master's house and part of the platform are all that remain. Retrace your steps to return to the start unless you have arranged a pick-up.

31 John Forrest Heritage Trail

Other walking trails within the John Forrest National Park

1. **The Glen Brook Dam Walk** – an easy 2 km walk
2. **The Wildflower Walk** – a 2 km walk that takes you through some of the parks best wildflower areas.
3. **The Eagle View Walk Trail** – a 15 km demanding trail that leads you out to the more remote areas of the park.

Lake Leschenaultia

Lake Leschenaultia is situated 40 kilometres northeast of Perth near the town of Chidlow. The lake was created in 1897 to provide water for the rail network that went from Midland and up onto the Darling Scarp. In 1948 the Shire of Mundaring took over the management of the area and it is now a popular leisure destination. Within the 168 hectares of the park it is possible to canoe, cycle, walk, swim, bird watch and BBQ. There is ample parking, sheltered picnic tables, a kiosk and a café. It is also possible to camp at the park by prior arrangement with the ranger. The park is open every day of the year, with the gates open 0830-1630; though it is possible to walk in after hours. There is an entry fee of $6.00 per car and no dogs are allowed.

There are two walks within the park area, both of which will give you a chance of seeing wildflowers, western grey kangaroos, possums, bandicoots, echidnas and native birds, depending on season and time of day.

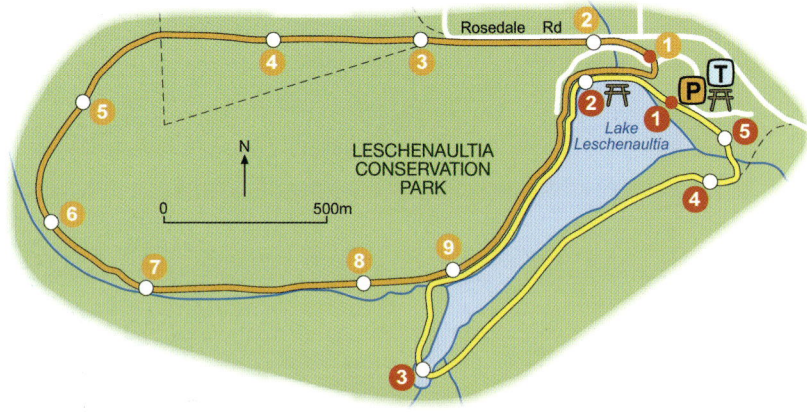

32 Lake Leschenaultia Lakeside Walk

At a glance

Grade: Easy

Time: 1 hr

Distance: 3 km circuit

Conditions: Suitable all year round, although spring is best for wildflowers

Getting there:

Bus: The 320 bus from Midland stops in Chidlow, then a 30 min walk to the park (signposted)

Car: Follow the Great Eastern Hwy past Mundaring and through Sawyers Valley, then turning left onto Old Northam Rd, left onto Thomas Rd and right onto Reservoir St – turn left at the end of this street onto Rosedale Rd; the picnic area is ahead on your left

Further Information:
www.mundaringtourism.com.au, T 9572 4248, see page 144 for map

32 Lake Leschenaultia Lakeside Walk

Walk directions

1 Begin close to the lower parts of the car park, where the beach and the dam wall meet and there is a sheltered picnic table. As you walk along the dam wall (keeping it to your left) you can see how the reservoir sits in its position between two sets of hills, which can be seen on the opposite shore and to your right. Below the dam wall on your right is a very shady picnic area that is very popular in summer, it also gives an indication of how deep the lake is.

2 At the end of the dam wall follow the track to the left and pass a series of small beaches and picnic sites. The forest trees come down to the lake shore and are comprised of jarrah (*Eucalyptus marginata*) and marri (*Eucalyptus calophylla*). In spring many different species of wildflower can be found growing in the undergrowth, including blue leschenaultias (*Leschenaultia biloba*) and white cottontop (*Conostylis setosa*). The area is also home to the brilliant blue-coloured splendid fairy wren (*Malurus splendens*) and welcome swallows (*Hirundo neoxena*) who feed on the insects that breed on the lake. Continue on past the reed beds, home to numerous species of water birds, to the far end of the lake where the reeds become much denser and the ground either side of the path more waterlogged. This makes for the ideal environment for the paperbark trees (*Melaleuca rhaphiophylla*) growing here.

3 As you circle the far end of the lake and walk back up the eastern shore there are a couple of places where there is a fork in the path: in each case take the left hand path that keeps you closest to the lake.

32 Lake Leschenaultia Lakeside Walk

4 At just past the 2 kilometre point there is a fenced crossroads. This was the site of a miniature railway track that was run as a tourist attraction some years ago. It was at this point the rail track crossed the walking path. Take the left turn.

5 400 metres further on there is a 'T' junction near the terminus of the railway. Again, take the left-hand turn. I walked this on a sunny spring morning and found a large goanna soaking up the sun's warmth. The marri and jarrah trees start to give way to wandoo (*Eucalyptus wandoo*), readily identified by their pale coloured powdery bark. At the eastern corner of the lake there are more reed beds and some orange wattle trees (*Acacia saligna*). You will also pass the shed that is the home to the canoe hire facility. On your right, set back among the trees, is the camping area. Continue walking along the lawned area and you will be back where you started at waypoint 1.

32 Lake Leschenaultia Lakeside Walk

33 Lake Leschenaultia Bush Walk

At a glance

Grade: Easy
Time: 2 hrs
Distance: 7.13 km circuit
Conditions: All year round, but best in spring for flora and fauna

Getting there:
Bus: The 320 bus from Midland stops in Chidlow, then a 30 min walk to the park (signposted)
Car: Follow the Great Eastern Hwy past Mundaring and through Sawyers Valley, then turning left onto Old Northam Rd, left onto Thomas Rd and right onto Reservoir St – turn left at the end of this street onto Rosedale Rd; the picnic area is ahead on your left

Further Information:
www.mundaringtourism.com.au,
T 9572 4248, see page 144 for map

33 Lake Leschenaultia Bush Walk

Walk directions

1 Start at the main park entrance and follow the road round the perimeter fence, heading in a westerly direction. As you walk through the car park you pass the spillway from the lake on your left. With a good winter rainfall there can be a substantial amount of water flowing down the waterway with its small waterfalls and cascades.

2 Just past the cascades there is a gate for after-hours access to the park; take the small narrow path just in front of it that heads down to the perimeter fence. You will come to a crossroads: to the left is the Mountain Bike track (MBT), to the right is a gate out of the park. Head straight on, and enter a marri forest. The marri is quite a distinctive tree with its rough flaky bark, and its large urn shaped fruit. If the bark is damaged it bleeds a very thick sticky red sap which gives the tree its common European name of red gum. A short way along on your right is another gate and to your left another turn off, keep going straight ahead.

3 The MBT crosses the walking path again here on your right – keep going straight on. On your right in the understory are Zamia Palms (*Macrozamia riedlei*). These were first observed by Europeans, on Wilhelm de Vlamingh's exploration of the Swan River in 1697, who reported becoming very ill after eating the palm nuts. For the local Nyoongar people the Zamia nuts are an important source of bush tucker and they have developed processes which remove the toxins allowing them to be eaten safely.

4 The MBT track intersects with the walking path, again carry straight on. Do the same for the next two instances where this occurs.

5 Just under 2 kilometres from the start there is a gate which restricts access to people who would illegally cut timber or who would use the park for motor sports, and provides access for emergency service vehicles. Continue along the main path in a southeasterly direction. Just past the gate there is a junction where (roughly in the middle of it) a gate that leads outside of the park, while on the other side of the track is a sign. Carry on walking straight ahead.

33 Lake Leschenaultia Bush Walk

6 At the 3-kilometre mark you reach an intersection on the trail. On your right is a small pedestrian gate near some rocks, while about 10 metres further on a larger gate allows vehicular access. Take the left turn opposite the pedestrian gate. There are several large clumps of red and green kangaroo paws (Anigozanthos manglesii) amongst the rocks on both sides of the fence.

7 Here you are 4 kilometres from the beginning: take the left-hand turn at the intersection and walk along the main trail for another 1.5 kilometres. You will come to a crossroads immediately followed by a 'Y' junction. Across the track is the No. 9 fire access gate. Go through the gate and take the right hand fork at the 'Y' junction. At this point you are now sharing the path with the MBT so exercise caution on all corners.

8 At the next intersection take the left-hand turn, leaving the MBT to the right. The marri forest is now giving way to wandoo. Up until recently wandoo was in much demand as it was highly prized for railway sleepers, bridge and wharf timber. In less than 100 metres there is a 'T' intersection with a sign pointing to the car park in both directions.

Take the left-hand turn back to the car park. You are now walking along the western bank of the lake.

9 The track divides here with the right-hand fork going over a small footbridge and taking you to the path along the dam wall. Follow this path and you will be back in the main car park.

34 The Mundaring Weir Rail Trail

The Mundaring Weir Rail Trail follows the spur line that was built from Mundaring to the construction site of the dam and initially carried just materials. Shortly after its completion the Weir became a popular tourist destination and a hotel was built by it to provide meals and accommodation for the visitors. The trail is a very popular one with both walkers and cyclists, and on a beautiful spring day it is very pleasant to walk down to the Weir, lunch at the hotel and walk back to Mundaring.

At a glance

Grade: Easy to medium
Time: 4 hrs
Distance: 7 km one way
Ascent/descent: 144 m ascent/descent
Conditions: Avoid in summer.
Getting there:
Bus: The 320 bus from Midland terminates in Craig St, one block away from the start of the walk
Car: Take the Great Eastern Hwy from the city heading east, travelling almost 14 km from Midvale; take a right onto Nichol St, right again onto Jacoby and left on both Gugeri and Phillips Rds to reach the park itself

Further Information:
www.mundaringtourism.com.au,
T 9572 4248

34 The Mundaring Weir Rail Trail

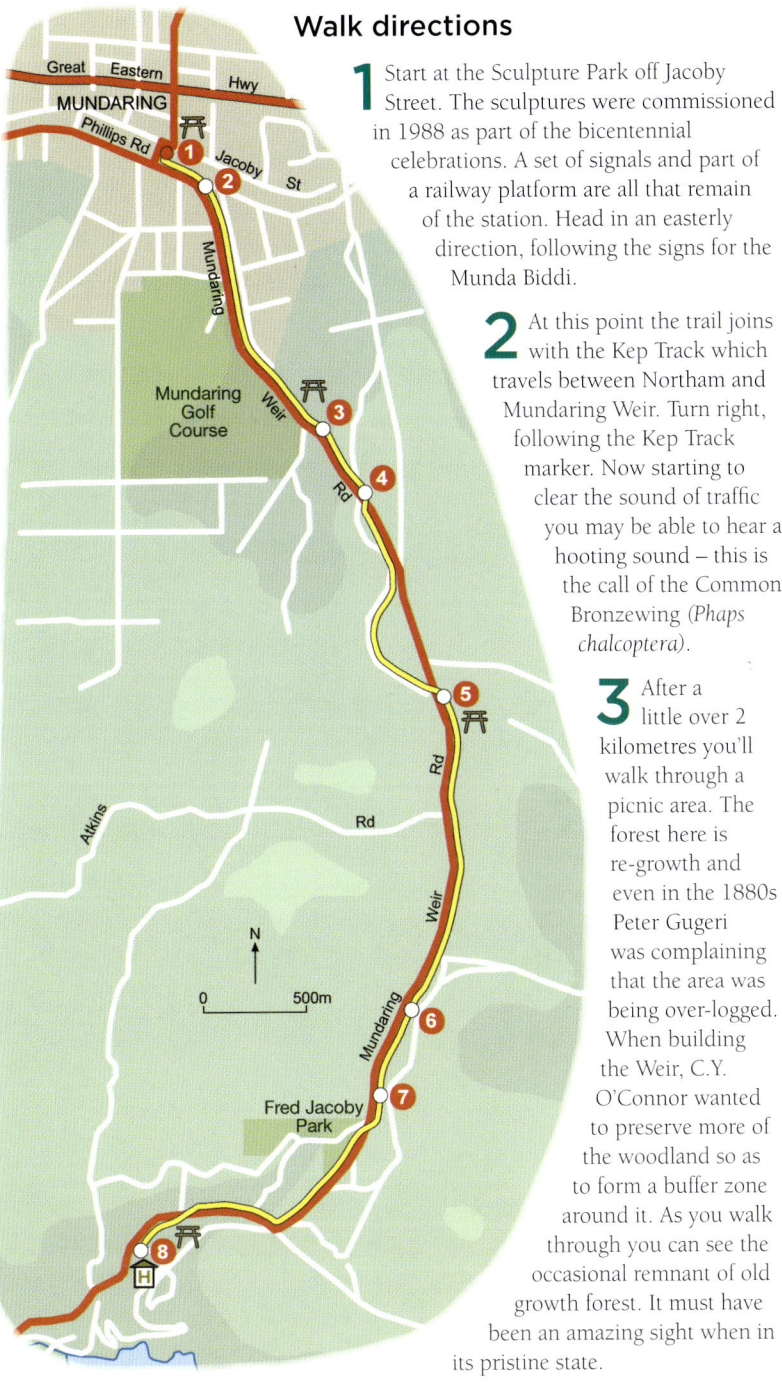

Walk directions

1 Start at the Sculpture Park off Jacoby Street. The sculptures were commissioned in 1988 as part of the bicentennial celebrations. A set of signals and part of a railway platform are all that remain of the station. Head in an easterly direction, following the signs for the Munda Biddi.

2 At this point the trail joins with the Kep Track which travels between Northam and Mundaring Weir. Turn right, following the Kep Track marker. Now starting to clear the sound of traffic you may be able to hear a hooting sound – this is the call of the Common Bronzewing (*Phaps chalcoptera*).

3 After a little over 2 kilometres you'll walk through a picnic area. The forest here is re-growth and even in the 1880s Peter Gugeri was complaining that the area was being over-logged. When building the Weir, C.Y. O'Connor wanted to preserve more of the woodland so as to form a buffer zone around it. As you walk through you can see the occasional remnant of old growth forest. It must have been an amazing sight when in its pristine state.

34 The Mundaring Weir Rail Trail

4 250 metres further on the track crosses Mundaring Weir Road. As you can see from the signage the track has a bit of an identity crisis: it's the Munda Biddi, the Kep and the Kattamorda. Take the trail over the gravel road – you are now on the site of Peter Gugeri's vineyard, St Bernard's – and back across Mundaring Weir Road, into the Grevillea Mycumbene picnic area.

5 Veer right as the path branches into two, going on to cross the Goldfields Water Supply Scheme pipeline and towards the site of the Number 2 Pumping Station. The remains of the wood-fuelled steam powered pump can be seen along with some sections of the old original pipe. It required the pressure from two pumps, the one here and the one at the Weir, to provide enough pressure to pump the water out of the Helena Valley and over the Darling Range. The two pumping stations were replaced by electric ones at the Weir in 1953, with this one being demolished some time later.

6 When you come to a fork in the trail, take the right branch as the other is for cyclists.

7 Cross Mundaring Weir Road and walk past the Fred Jacoby National Park. A little further on

34 The Mundaring Weir Rail Trail

there is a road junction with a roundabout; cross over and continue to follow the Kep Track markers.

8 About ten minutes later you should arrive at the Mundaring Weir Hotel. If you have no pre-arranged pick-up, you can either retrace your steps or take the Mundaring Weir Loop Trail back to the Sculpture Park (however, this was closed at the time of writing, so enquire at the Perth Hills District Office of the Department of Environment and Conservation, near Fred Jacoby Park as to whether it's open).

Perth history - Mundaring

The first European explorer of the area around Mundaring was Ensign Dale in 1829, but it was not until 1870 that the earliest recorded settlement was founded by a convict road party which camped there. Peter Gugeri, an Italian born in London, took up 48 hectares in 1882 and established a vineyard which he named St. Bernard, currently the location of the Weir Valley Farm. In 1894 a railway siding was built to service the timber industry and Jacoby renamed the siding Mundaring, having learnt that that was the Nyoongar name meaning "high place on a high place". In 1898 Mundaring was declared a townsite and by 1900 John Chipper (owner of the Mundaring Hotel) set about promoting the town as a tourist resort – "nature in its primitive state" was his marketing slogan. By 1914 it was fashionable to have a weekender in Mundaring and soon after people began to live there full-time and commuted to jobs in Perth by train.

35 The Golden Pipeline Trail

Tracing the history of the Goldfields Water Supply Scheme, this walk is a combination of two others: the Weir Walk and the O'Connor Trail. The Supply Scheme was an audacious plan to carry fresh water via a pipeline from the Darling Range to the Goldfields of Western Australia 560 kilometres to the east. The man commissioned to undertake this daunting task was the mercurial but brilliant Charles Yelverton O'Connor, the then

Engineer in Chief of Western Australia. Work commenced in 1896 and was completed in 1903. Tragically, O'Connor committed suicide before it was completed, whereupon it became the longest fresh water pipeline in the world and the dam the highest overflow dam in the world. This walk takes you through each of the scheme's three key elements:

1. The damming of the Helena River
2. The laying of the 760 mm diameter pipe
3. The construction of the eight pumping stations and the infrastructure needed to serve them

At a glance

Grade: Medium
Time: 2.5 hrs
Distance: 7 km return
Ascent/descent: 168 m ascent/descent
Conditions: Trail is well-signposted and with a lot of steps; avoid in summer

Getting there:

Car: Follow the Great Eastern Highway to Mundaring and then follow the signs to the Weir (there is parking outside Mundaring Weir Hall, or at the nearby Fred Jacoby Park)

Further Information:

www.keptrack.com.au/Weir_to_Mundaring.html, T 9295 2244 (Perth Hills National Park Centre), 9321 6088 (National Trust Western Australia)

35 The Golden Pipeline Trail

Walk directions

1 Outside the Mundaring Weir Hall (now an art gallery) there are several information signs for the Kep Track, the Weir Walk and the O'Connor Trail. Cross over Hall Road as if to go to the Mundaring Weir Hotel, but walk through the garden following the pipe on your left. After 100 metres at the bottom of the garden is a concrete bridge that crosses the pipe; go over it and cross both lanes of Weir Village Road. Turn right and follow the Kep Track markers through the picnic area and past the rose garden. Continue through the car park in a westerly direction – you will see a large information sign with a map of the Weir and, next to it, a sign pointing in the direction of the dam wall and the memorial, follow it.

2 Head down the steep steps and cross the road, following the Kep markers into another garden area. The Weir became a very popular tourist destination in the early part of the 20th century, especially when it overflowed – it did this more frequently then as the dam wall was lower. A garden of imported exotic plants was established with the aim of reminding visitors of 'home'.

3 At the monument to C.Y. O'Connor turn right and go down the steps and then walk across the dam wall to the other side of the Helena Valley.

4 At the end of the dam, turn right, walking past the toilet block and across the parking spaces. Walk through the picnic area at the base of the dam wall. It is here that you can begin to comprehend the sheer magnitude of the scale of the project. Cross the bridge over the spillway to get to the Number 1 Pumping Station (there is a museum inside it), pass it and follow the path around to your right.

5 At the Valve House climb the steps that take you back up to the dam wall. Follow the gravel drive at the top that bends off to left and you will come out beneath some granite outcrops. Keep walking towards the trees straight ahead of you and you reach the pipeline. On your right the path goes between some boulders and past the Black Cockatoos painted on the pipe. Cross over the pipe on the steps and then continue walking between the two pipes until you reach the hotel. Walk past the hall and follow the trail markers up to the roundabout.

35 The Golden Pipeline Trail

6 Cross over Mundaring Weir Road and continue past Fred Jacoby Park on your left. Just past the Department of Environment and Conservation office and the top entry for Fred Jacoby Park, cross over Mundaring Weir Road and continue to the site of the Number 2 Pumping Station.

7 Take the trail to the right and up some steps, following the Kep Trail markers with a green stripe. At the top of the steps turn right. At length the Kep Trail leaves the gravel road via a turn-off on your left. When the track divides, take the right hand fork.

8 After 200 metres you'll enter a clearing with a stream, lots of grass trees and a picnic bench. Walk through and straight over the crossroads. This next section of the walk takes you through some of the loveliest forest in the hills. The mixed jarrah and marri re-growth, with an undergrowth of grass trees and zamia palms, has a veritable carpet of wildflowers in spring. After walking under some overhead power lines the Kep Track merges with the Bibbulmun Track - turn right.

9 A short while later there is a boot cleaning station. This is there to prevent the spread of dieback, so please use it. Carry on towards the Hills Forest Centre, then cross the parking area to arrive at group of buildings. The Kep continues to your left between two of the buildings. Follow

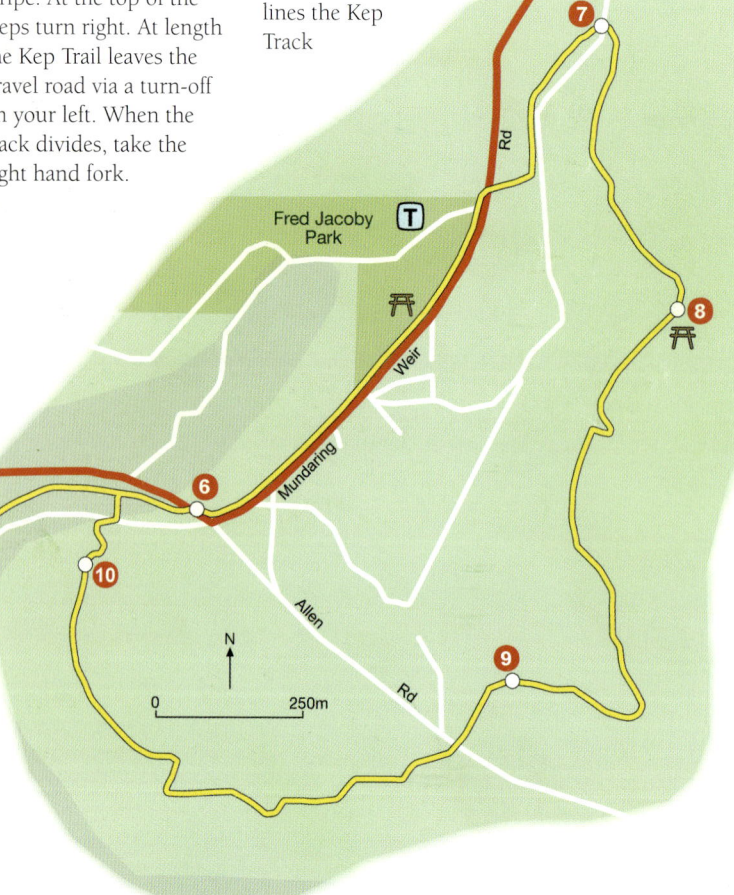

35 The Golden Pipeline Trail

the Bibbulmun markers as they are clearer at this point. The path weaves through the trees and goes down a series of flights of steps. After 600 metres you'll come to a lookout with views over Lake C.Y. O'Connor and the Weir.

10 Continue to follow the Kep Track markers along a wide trail, past the gate to a bed and breakfast and down some more steps. 600 metres on from the lookout you will be back at Weir Village Road. Cross over, go down another set of steps and turn left at the bottom. This takes you back to Mundaring Weir Hall.

36 Paten's Brook Track

Beelu National Park, formerly Mundaring National Park, provides the backdrop to this walk, beginning at the Perth Hills National Parks Centre. Within the park it is possible to see chuditch (western quoll), the quenda (southern brown bandicoot), common bushtail possum, short-beaked echidna, western grey kangaroo and the western brush wallaby. On the northern side of the loop it is the typical forest of the Darling Range: jarrah and marri with grasstrees, bull banksia, zamia and sheoak. On the southern side the track passes through the state pine plantation and the contrast between the two ecosystems is striking. Unfortunately the walk passes through a section of dieback-infested forest so walkers must clean their shoes at the designated cleaning stations.

At a glance

Grade: Medium
Time: 3 hrs
Distance: 9 km circuit
Ascent/descent: 94 m ascent/descent
Conditions: Avoid in summer

Getting there:

Car: From Mundaring drive south on the Mundaring Weir Rd, turning left onto Allen Rd just before the Weir –Perth Hills National Parks Centre is located on the right

Further Information:
www.perthtourism.com.au/standard-pg-1180.asp,
T 9295 2244

36 Paten's Brook Track

Walk directions

1 The start of the trail follows the Bibbulmun Track out of the centre. Walk to the rearmost part of the car park and look for the main sign for the Bibbulmun next to a sign for the Cockatoo Care program. At the sign turn left and follow the yellow triangular wagyl markers.

2 After 10 or so minutes of walking, the path passes under some power lines and crosses over the service road. As you walk through the forest you pass a series of information boards talking about the significance of fire and its effect on the forest. The forest in Beelu National Park undergoes prescribed burn offs in a checkerboard pattern and it is interesting to observe how the forest responds to the various stages of burn off and regeneration. Cross straight over at the crossroads.

3 Turn left at an intersection. At length you will need to leave the Bibbulmun Track, which goes off to your left, and start following the Paten's Brook Track markers instead – these have a white triangle with two green gum leaves. At just over 2 kilometres from the start there are the remains of a large tree which has been hollowed out by fire. Keep walking for another 450 metres and take the turning on the right.

4 Keep walking downhill and you come to Paten's Brook Campsite. This is a fee paying site (call 9295 2244 to book) and has 12 camping spots, a water tank and a toilet block. There is no camping between 1st November and 31st March, which is the peak bushfire season in which a total fire ban is in force. Amongst the grass trees by the toilet are cowslip orchids which may be seen from July to early December. Turn right and follow the track along the valley, taking the right hand turn 350 metres further along.

5 Ignore the turn off to your right and continue straight; at this point the track runs parallel to Paten's Brook. After a few minutes the trail passes under some

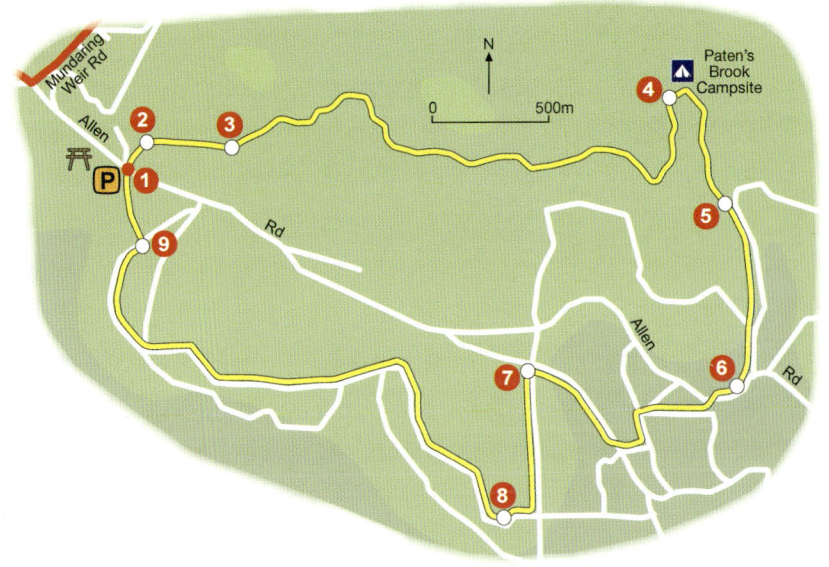

36 Paten's Brook Track

more power lines before meeting up with a partially asphalted road. Turn right onto the road.

6 After 200 metres take the left turn and walk for another 30 metres before turning right into the pine plantation. As you walk through the plantation you can see that there is a thick mulch of pine needles on the forest floor, and very little understory. There is also the strong scent of pine resin. Walk for about 5-6 minutes and then take the left-hand turn. In another 120 metres, at the junction with the partially demolished humpy, turn right. In 15 minutes or so you will pass a sign that says when the stand of pine trees was planted – take the right turn here.

7 Turn left at this point, then left again, heading down towards Lake C.Y. O'Connor; after 80 meters turn right at the junction.

8 Keep going for another 200 metres, continuing straight on through all crossroads.

9 After about 10 minutes take the left-hand turn, then after 140 metres turn left onto the road. At this point you are approximately 200 metres from the Perth Hills Centre's car park.

36 Paten's Brook Track

Staying found in Beelu National Park

Over the years I have encountered a lot of walkers who say they found themselves lost while in this area and yet DEC are very solicitous in their trail marking. People may lose their way for a couple of reasons; firstly, according to the rangers, a lot of visitors and walkers souvenir the trail markers. If you find that markers are missing please inform the staff at the centre and they will rectify it. The second reason is that walkers become pre-occupied with the scenery or are deep in thought or conversation. So if you should find yourself temporarily lost, re-trace your steps until you find a trail marker. The *worst* thing you can do is to leave the trail and bush bash to where you think you should be. The forest in the Darling Ranges often appears to be quite featureless and this makes navigation by sight and memory difficult at the least and extremely dangerous at the worst.

37 Rocky Pool

The Kalamunda National Park covers 375 hectares of bushland and it is notable for it diversity of fauna and flora. This walk follows Piesse Brook to a large rock pool at the base of a waterfall. The valley sides are covered in open woodland comprised of jarrah, marri and wandoo. The pool is the perfect spot to sit and contemplate the sound of the flowing water and the songs of the native birds around it. Piesse Brook was named after the policeman and magistrate William Roper Piesse who arrived in the Swan River Colony in 1842. Note that sign posting on the trail is very irregular.

At a glance

Grade: Easy
Time: 1 hr
Distance: 4.7 km return
Conditions: Avoid in summer
Getting there:
Public Transport: Nearest bus stop is 3.7 km away from the trail head
Car: Take Mundaring Rd out of Kalamunda, turn left onto Humerston Rd and then left into Schipp Rd
Further Information: www.naturebase.net, T 9295 2244

37 Rocky Pool

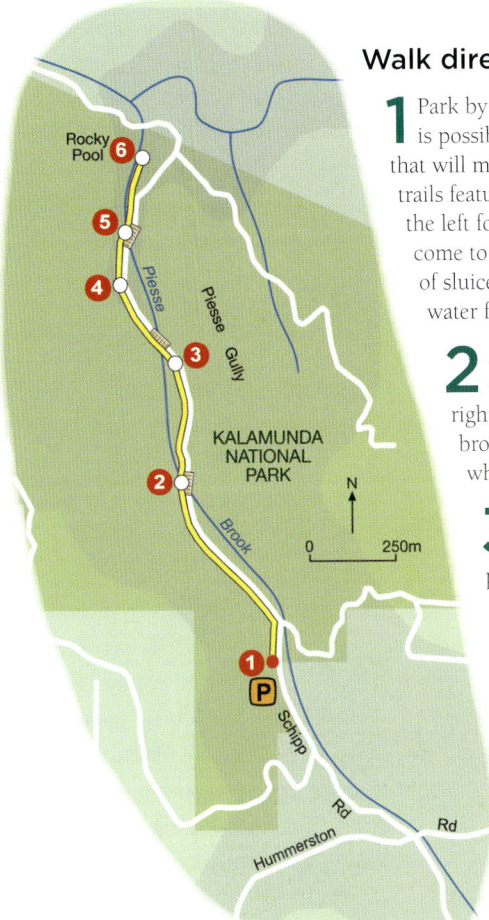

Walk directions

1 Park by the first sign in the car park - it is possible to drive in even further but that will mean you will miss on some of the trails features. After about 200 meters take the left fork in the trail, and you'll then come to a part of the brook where a series of sluice gates were used to control the water flow.

2 About 160 meters further on cross over the brook to your right. Veer left once over, keeping the brook on your left. Keep going past when you reach a gate.

3 500 metres from the car park is the gate to the national park, go through and keep walking along the track. At the next junction keep going straight ahead back across the brook.

4 After roughly 1 kilometre there is a crossroads. The way to the rock pool is straight ahead, but it is worth taking a brief side trip down to the brook on your right to look at the wild flowers and the brook itself.

37 Rocky Pool

5 At the next concrete bridge cross the brook once more and keep going. After a further kilometre or so there is a small track off to your left, this takes you down to the pool. There's a tree with a blue arrow marker right by the turn off.

6 At the rock pool, depending upon the water level, it is possible to walk around, but be careful in wet weather as the rocks are very slippery. To return to your car re-trace your steps.

38 Lesmurdie Falls

The Lesmurdie Brook flows through the centre of Lesmurdie National Park and tumbles 50 metres over the sheer face of the Darling Scarp. In winter, when rains swell the brook, the waterfall pours over the stream's granite bedrock. On a clear day, from lookout points on the steep walkways that wander through the park, the flat land of the coastal plain sweeps out over Perth city to Rottnest Island on the western horizon. The walk can also be done in reverse by parking at the Palm Terrace entrance to Lesmurdie National Park in Wattle Grove.

At a glance

Grade: Medium
Time: 25 mins
Distance: 2 km return
Ascent/descent: 119 m ascent/descent
Conditions: Avoid in summer – paths well made and signposted
Getting there:
Bus: The 282 stops on George Rd, 1.9 km away
Car: Go along Welshpool Rd East from Peter Rd, turn left onto Lesmurdie Road and then left onto Falls Rd – the car park is some distance ahead on your right (to find the other end of the trail, turn from the Tonkin Hwy onto Hale Rd/Hatwin Rd, right onto Anderson Rd, left onto Lewis Rd and right onto Palm Tce – the parking lot is at the end of the terrace)

Further Information:
www.naturebase.net

38 Lesmurdie Falls

Walk directions

1 The car park is at the head of the trail – walk through the BBQ and picnic area and follow the signs for Lesmurdie Falls and Palm Terrace. After 50 metres, and just past two picnic tables, the trail divides. Take the left hand fork.

2 At this point you should come across a bridge – ignore it and keep following the path instead. Ahead there are two lookout platforms giving views of the falls and the Swan Coastal Plain below.

3 Head along the path for another 140 metres – you are now able to look back at the falls. They are an impressive sight in spring with the water cascading over the red granite and contrasting with the brilliant green of the vegetation and the deep blue of the sky. When you reach a wooden bridge you will have another view, this time over the city to where the Bank West and Central Park buildings dominate the CBD skyline. Looking out to the opposite hillside you can see woodland made up of marri, karri and grass trees.

4 The trail now follows a steep water gully down the hill. Either side of the narrow path is a thick hedge of native shrubs and bushes, and on a warm spring day there is the persistent hum of bees pollinating the plants

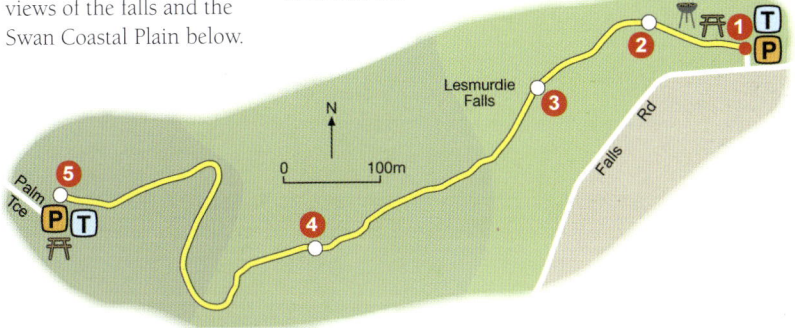

38 Lesmurdie Falls

and butterflies sunning themselves. At the bottom of the gully you come to a sign for the Lesmurdie National Park. There is a very convenient bench under some trees by the brook. Turn left here to follow the path.

5 It is worth spending a bit of time at Palm Terrace car park, firstly to prepare for the climb back up the hill, and secondly just to observe the tremendous variety of bird life. You may see Western King Parrots (also known as the Red Capped Parrot) feeding in the marri trees. Return along the same route to get back to your car.

38 Lesmurdie Falls

39 The Mason and Bird Heritage Trail

In the 1860s Benjamin Mason founded a timber exporting business based on the Canning River at what is now Mason's Landing. This walking trail follows part of the route of the company's wooden horse-drawn tramway, which linked the mill in Kalamunda and the company's base on the Canning, where the timber was then sent down river to Fremantle prior to being exported to India for use as railway sleepers. The trail now passes through a water catchment and this has allowed the bush to regenerate, becoming an important conservation area, particularly for Black Cockatoos.

At a glance

Grade: Medium
Time: 2 hrs
Distance: 8 km one way
Ascent/descent: 156 m ascent
Conditions: Avoid during summer
Getting there:
Bus: The 230 bus stops at the corner of Maddington and Dellar Rds – walk up Maddington Rd to Hardinge Rd
Car: Turn off the Albany Hwy into Kelvin Rd, right into Maddington Rd and continue into Hardinge Rd, stopping at the picnic area on your left
Further Information: T 9398 2551 (City of Gosnells Heritage Officer)

39 The Mason and Bird Heritage Trail

Walk directions

1 From the BBQ and picnic area and walk up past the outdoor recreation centre. In the cul de sac two trails have their starting point. One is the Kattamorda Heritage Trail, which is through the white gate, the other is the Mason and Bird Trail which is on your right behind a barrier of boulders. Take the Mason and Bird trail. Soon you will enter the Bickley area, which is covered in a heap of trails and tracks. These are used by horse riders, mountain bikers, orienteers and other outdoor enthusiasts. Keep on the main track unless directed otherwise. The bush on either side of the track is home to fairy blue wrens and the brilliantly coloured males are easy to spot.

2 Here you will reach a place locally known as Shoofly Hill (the name is spray painted on one of the rocks in yellow). The trail now joins the Kattamorda Track and follows it for a while. This section is also the access road for the New Victoria Dam, so be aware that vehicles also use it. Ahead on your left is the site of the old Boys Brigade Camp – nothing much remains now, just the concrete and brick foundations for the ablutions block. Further on, at the 1.3 kilometre mark, you reach the Munday Brook Timber Tramway Bridge.

3 This original wandoo and jarrah bridge was built in 1871 by the Mason and Bird Timber Company using ticket-of-leave convict labour. The bridge was restored in 1989 as part of a Commonwealth Bicentennial Project. Just over the bridge the Water Corporations service road turns off to the right. Follow the Mason and Bird

39 The Mason and Bird Heritage Trail

Track as it carries straight on up the hill. In the paddocks on your left you can hear a stream flowing; if you walk down the slope you will find the stream plus a wonderful display of Arum Lilies (*Zantedeschia aethiopica*) – although these are now considered a noxious pest they do make for a splendid spectacle.

4 On the right at this point are the remains of kaolin pits, used in local ceramic and porcelain industries. As you go on the track starts to level out and just up ahead is a gate across it. Just before the gate is a sign on a tree on the right hand side of the path, pointing to the right at a path that goes up into the trees.

5 Follow the path to the right. At length it opens out into a car park by the gate of the Victoria Dam. Turn right and follow the road towards the dam.

6 Continue down the road until on the left hand side you come across the gravesite of Francis Watson, who died at the age of two days in 1876, around which time there was quite a settlement for the timber workers, with areas given over to growing fruit and vegetables to feed them. This is the end point of the walk; to return just retrace your steps unless you have pre-arranged a pick-up.

40 Sixty Foot Falls

Ellis Brook flows in winter and spring and cascades down the Sixty Foot Falls before flowing into the Canning River. Ellis Brook Valley is one of the best wildflower areas in Perth, with some 550 species of flowering plant. The peak time to visit the park is between July and October when the Brook is flowing and the wildflowers put on a riotous display of colour. There are three other walks in the park and details of these are given on the information board near the entrance.

At a glance

Grade: Hard
Time: 45 mins
Distance: 2 km circuit
Ascent/descent: 124 m ascent/descent
Conditions: Avoid in summer – this is a challenging walk on an irregular surface

Getting there:

Train/Bus: Catch the train to Seaforth Station, then walk to Albany Hwy and catch the 220 bus, get off after Ferres Dr (stop no. 10021) and walk the 3.9 km to the park

Car: Take the Tonkin Hwy, turning east into Gosnells Rd East, right into Pitt Rd, right into Hayward Rd, left into Quarry Rd and left into Rushton Rd, continuing to the park at the end of the road

Further Information: T 9391 3222
http://tiny.cc/ellis_brook_brochure

40 Sixty Foot Falls

Walk directions

1 Start at the picnic bench at the far end of the car park.

2 A short way along the trail there is a fork in the path. Veer right, keeping the brook on your left. As you walk, the shrubs and bushes form a virtual tunnel covered in wildflowers - be careful if you brush against them as they are likely to be full of bees. Another 200 metres on and you will reach the first viewing platform, and from here you will get your first glimpse of the falls if they are flowing. Carry on another 270 metres to a fork in the path. The left fork takes you down to the brook while the path to the right continues to the top of the hill. It is worth going down to the brook to see the rock pools and the plant life that surrounds them.

3 Carry on up the hill to viewing platform number two. By now you will have climbed 60 metres in a short distance, so this is a good place to admire the view and catch your breath.

4 From here follow the path to another fork in the trail. Take the right turn. Ahead, at a point 630 metres from the start, you will have reached the top of the falls. Be careful as you walk around on the rock as it is slippery in wet weather.

5 The track continues on your right. Step over the brook and there is a trail marker – follow it. Eventually you will reach a point where several trails merge. Keep going on the main wide trail.

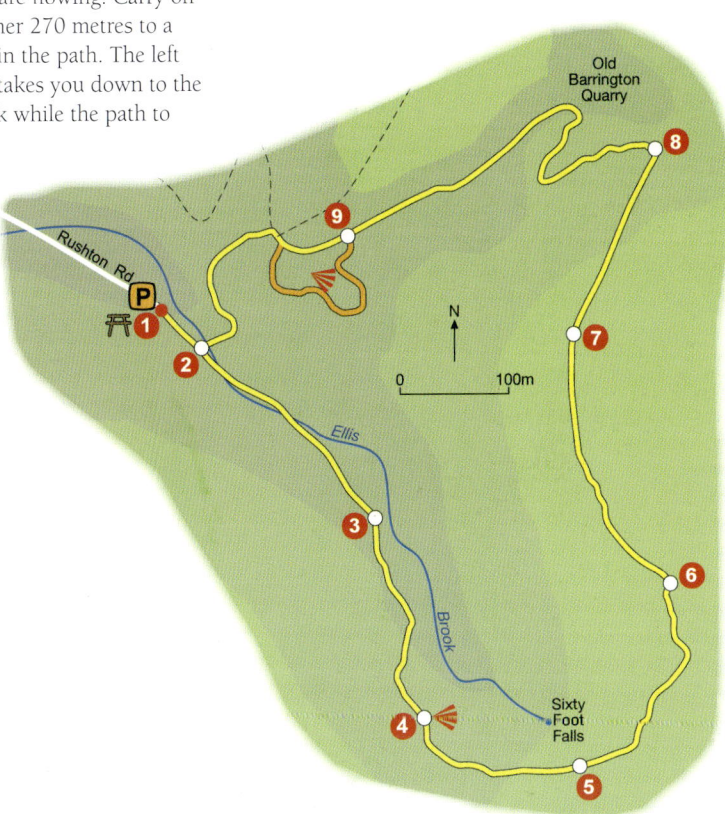

40 Sixty Foot Falls

6 From this point you will climb to the highest point on the walk at 200 metres – and it is all downhill from here! On your right is a stand of rare salmon white gum trees (*Eucalyptus lane-poolei*). These are a handsome variety of eucalypt which have pale orange powdery or white bark, long tapering green leaves, orange flower buds and creamy white flowers.

7 At a point 1.2 kilometres from the start there is a junction, and straight ahead is the fence for the old Barrington Quarry, which was operational in the 1950s and early 1960s. It was used for some time as a popular swimming hole known as 'the rockies' (now fenced off for safety reasons) and is now a popular destination for abseilers and climbing groups. On your left are some steps which will take you down the hill – follow these. The path now basically follows the edge of the quarry and at times follows the boundary fence.

8 Follow the quarry service road out of the quarry, walking across the large open area, at the far side of which you will come to some wooden posts and railings. There is a gap between them with some steps going down, follow this track.

9 The path divides at this point; and you have an opportunity to take a side-trip to lookout number three. If you choose to do so you can either retrace your steps back to the path and turn left, or carry on the loop trail back to the main path. Once on the main path continue straight, going down the steps and across the bridge. Turn right immediately after the bridge and the path takes you back to the car park where you started.

40 Sixty Foot Falls

41 Mount Dale Circuit

Back in 1829 the Swan Colony was in a bad shape and was in danger of starving, so Governor Stirling packed Ensign Robert Dale off to discover pastures new. Dale found a way up and over the Darling Scarp via the Helena Valley and consequently "discovered" the Avon Valley. As he went on his journey he named various places and features after his superiors, family and friends, however, on his way back he ran out of names and so named Mount Dale after himself. This walk, in St Helena National Park, circumnavigates the peak and rewards walkers with panoramic views of the surrounding area. In spring the area is blessed with an over abundance of wildflowers, especially on the edges of the granite outcrops. Birdwatchers will see quite a variety of different birds including wedged tailed eagles. Unfortunately the walk can be difficult to follow in places due to vandals destroying the trail markers. Also be careful driving along Ashendon Road, particularly on the blind corners.

At a glance

Grade: Easy
Time: 1 hour
Distance: 2.3 km circuit
Ascent/descent: 72 m ascent/descent
Conditions: Avoid in summer; well maintained trails; signage can be poor

Getting there:

Car: Drive for 47 km out of Kelmscott on the Brookton Hwy, turn into Ashendon Rd and drive for 6 km, turn into Mount Dale Rd and this takes you straight up to the top of the hill

Further Information:
http://tiny.cc/mount_dale,
T 9295 2244

41 Mount Dale Circuit

Walk directions

1 Park in the upper car park and enjoy the view - at an elevation of 539 meters you can look out over a lot of forest and take heart in the fact that you have been able to drive up to it! At the railings turn left and follow the path. After 100 meters the path divides, take the right branch and 20 meters further on turn right again.

2 The radio mast is the highest point at 546 meters. There used to be a fire watchtower here, and as you walked round the back of the radio tower you may notice the concrete footings for it. Turn right and follow the wide track down to the white gate. Go through and turn right onto the gravel road and follow it down.

3 Turn into the picnic area and walk towards the toilet, just before you get there the trail turns to the left. There should be a trail marker here but it often gets vandalized and/or pulled up. Do not be in too much of a hurry to scoot off as among the boulders are lots of different species of wildflower, some of which only grow on granite outcrops.

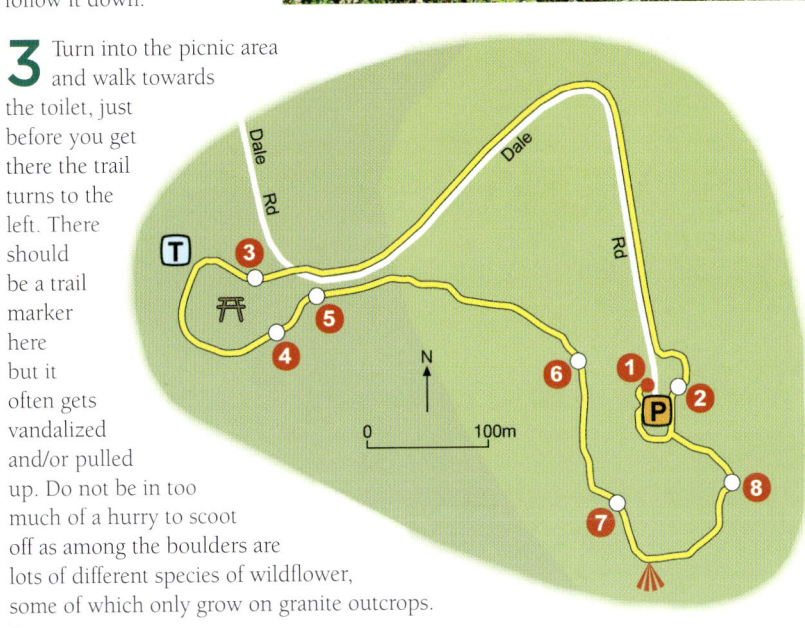

41 Mount Dale Circuit

4 At the crossroads: if the trail marker is there follow it, but if you cannot keep walking straight ahead, up some steps and past a picnic bench.

5 The trail narrows and passes through some thick parrot bush. After a short while it takes you to the road and then turns right, running alongside it.

6 On the granite dome hold the contour line and skirt the upper edge for 100 meters, at which point the vegetation starts to close round the path again. The trail heads off down to your right.

7 The path winds around the hill and gives you views of the hills to the south. Keep following the path to the left.

8 Take the next two left turns and you will find yourself back at the upper car park.

42 Abyssinia Rock

This is a very popular walk and it is very easy to see why; it is very easy to follow, with an open jarrah and marri forest, home to a wide variety of fauna and flora. The views from the top of the rock extend from the southeast to the southwest of the Darling Range. Abyssinia Rock itself is covered with mosses and lichens which create interesting patterns and textures – they are also very fragile and take many years to regenerate so try not to walk over them. Lizards sun themselves on the rock, but at the merest hint of danger they dart for the cover of the numerous cracks and crevices that cover the surface. As you walk on the rock you can hear and feel that some sections are hollow. The constant expansion and contraction caused by changes in heat and cold mean that sheets of rock are peeled off of the surface, and the hollowness is the air pocket between the sheet and the base rock. Dog lovers should note that the area is regularly baited with 1080 poison – do not bring dogs!

At a glance

Grade: Medium
Time: 3 hrs
Distance: 10.3 km return
Ascent/descent: 96 m ascent/descent
Conditions: Avoid in summer
Getting there:
Car: 20 km past Karragullen on the Brookton Highway
Further Information:
www.bibbulmuntrack.org.au/track-info.aspx, T 9481 0551

42 Abyssinia Rock

Walk directions

1 Look for the Bibbulmun Track trail markers; they are a yellow triangle with a black waugal (rainbow serpent). As you face south standing in the car park there are two tracks: the first one closest to the road is the service road for the power lines, the second is the Bibbulmun Track. When the trail divides, take the right hand fork and follow the path uphill.

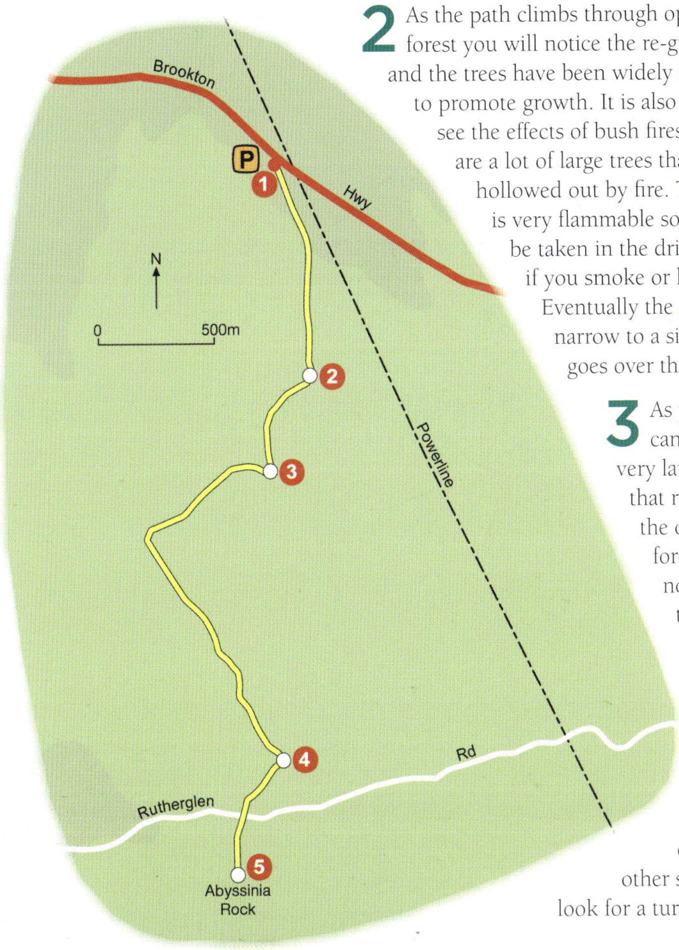

2 As the path climbs through open jarrah forest you will notice the re-growth forest and the trees have been widely spaced out to promote growth. It is also possible to see the effects of bush fires, and there are a lot of large trees that have been hollowed out by fire. The bush here is very flammable so care must be taken in the drier months if you smoke or light a fire. Eventually the path will narrow to a single track as it goes over the hill.

3 As you pass you can see some very large jarrah trees that remain from the old growth forest. They were not logged as their shape or configuration made them unsuitable for turning into lumber. As you descend the other side of the hill look for a turning onto a

42 Abyssinia Rock

wide track on your left. The forest becomes denser and as the path leads you to a junction take the right hand turn.

4 After five or six minutes you come out on Rutherglen Road. Cross over and follow the Bibbulmun Track markers through the grass trees on the other side, keeping a look out for a small cairn, or pile of stones on your left. A series of cairns will mark a pathway to the summit.

5 This is the end of the outward leg. To return to your car retrace your journey.

42 Abyssinia Rock

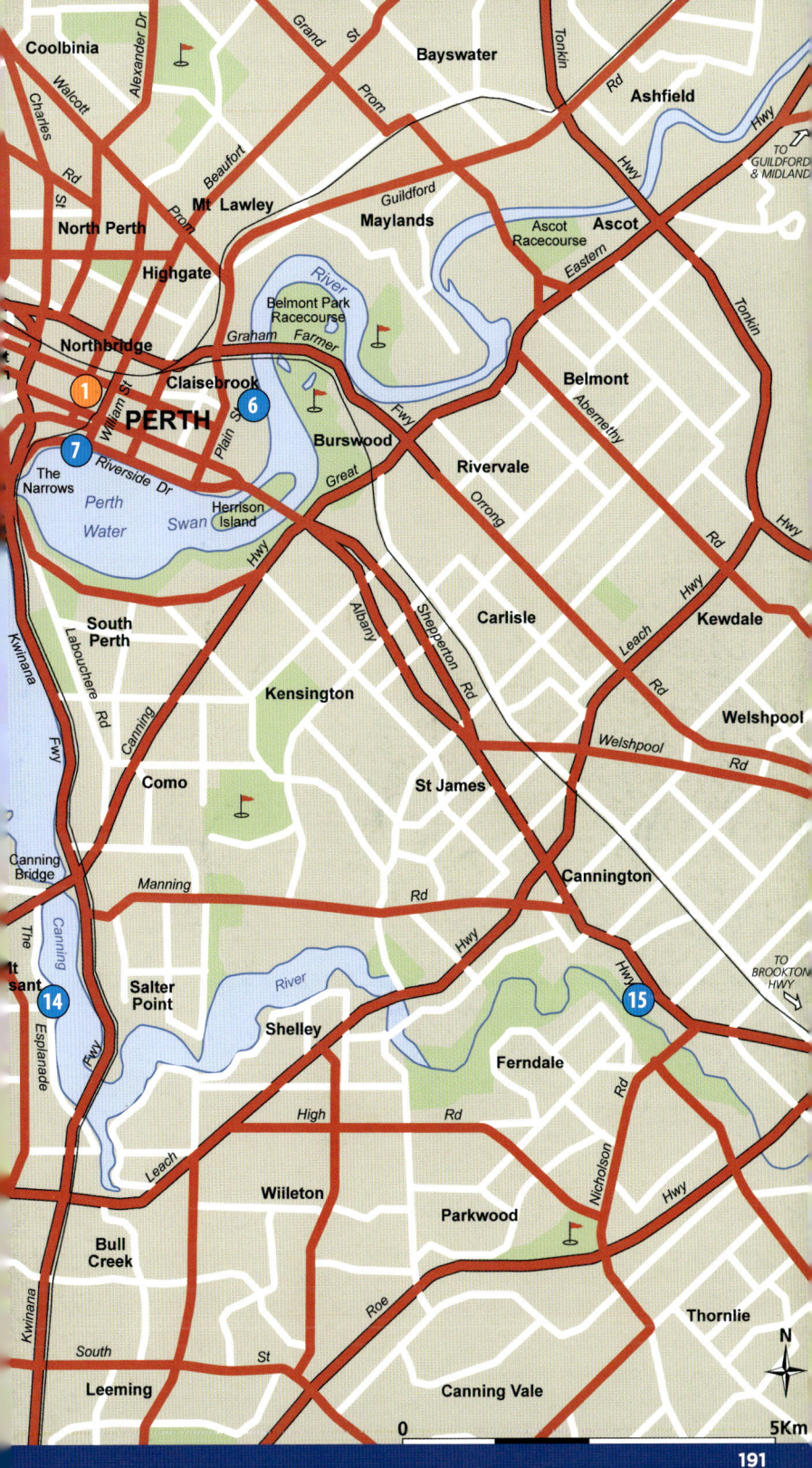

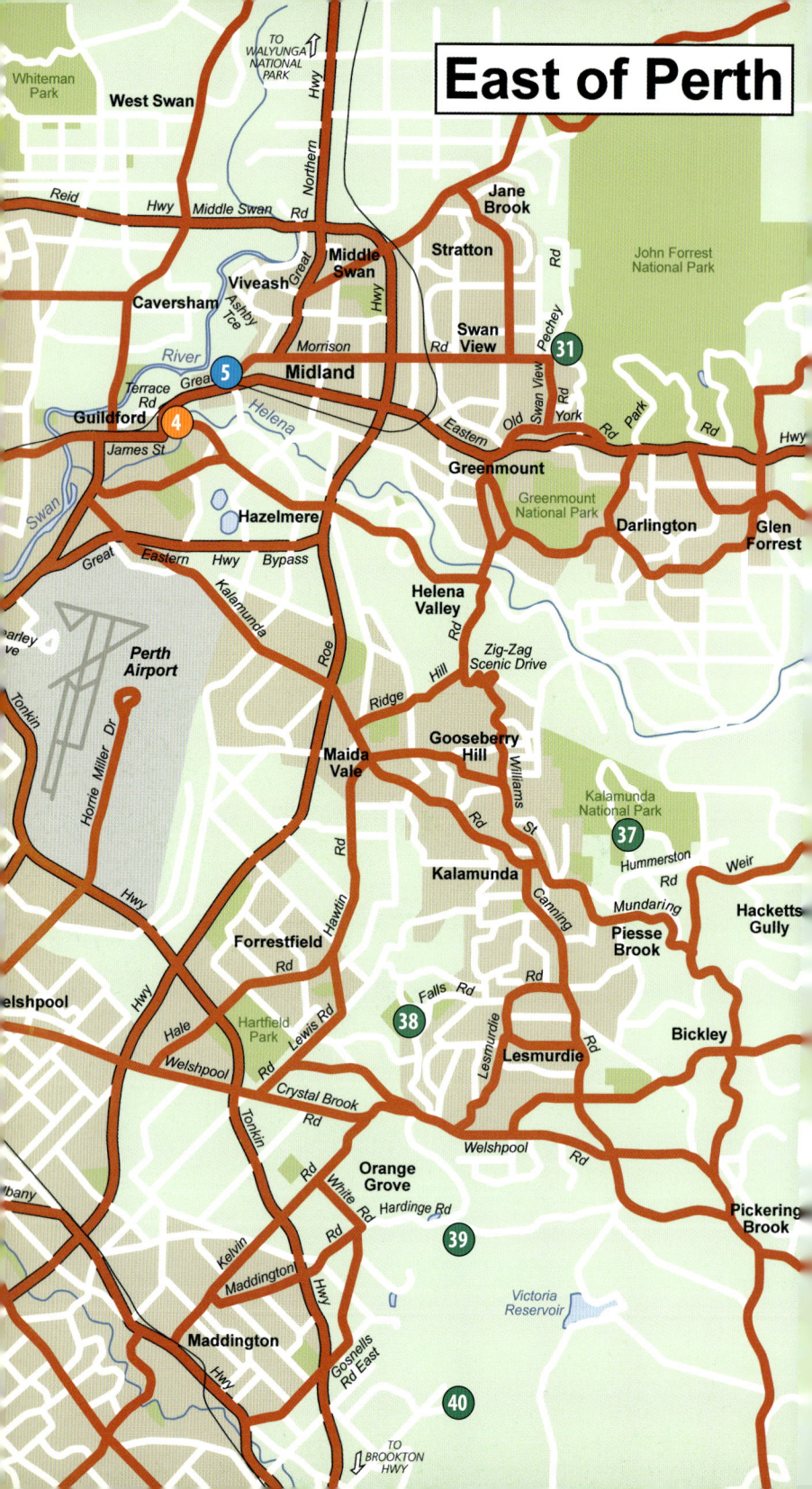

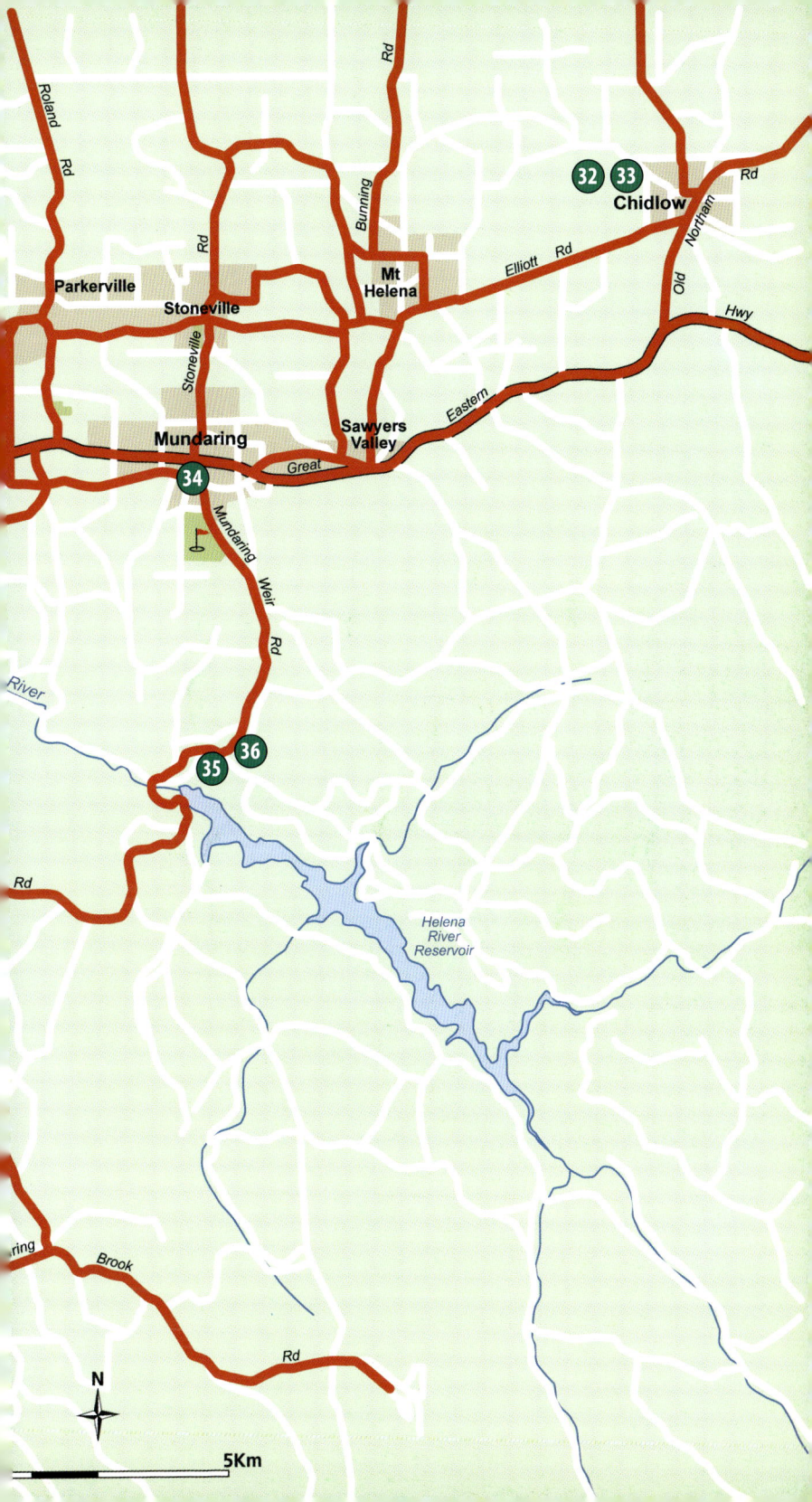

Index

A
Aboriginal Heritage Trail, 138
Abyssinia Rock, 184-187
Alan Green Conservatory, 15
Amateur Rowing Ass. Of WA, 69
Ambler, Syd, 138
Avon Descent, 138
Avon Valley, 58

B
Bailey, Claire, 14
bain, 97-98
Bali Bombing Memorial, 16
Bank West Building, 13
Barrack Street Jetty, 41
Barracks Arch, 17
Barrington Quarry, 178
Batavia shipwreck, 67
Baudin, Nicholas, 51, 75
Beeliar people, 48
Beeliar Wetlands, 77, 96-99
Beelu National Park, 160-163
Bernales, Claude de, 14
Bibbulmun nation, 36
Bibbulmun Track, 158-159, 161, 185-186
Bibbulmun Yorga, 87
bird observation tower, 45
Bird, Francis, 73
Bishop's Gerdens, 15
Blackies, 48
Blackwall Reach Lookout, 49
Blood on Borneo, 128
Bon Scott Memorial, 24
Botanic Garden, 19
Burns, Shirley, 71
Butler, John, 52

C
Camps at Canning Bridge, 71
Canning Bridge, 68-69
Canning River - history, 75
Canning River Regional Park, 72-75
Canning, George, 75
Cape Peron, 122-125
Catalpa Memorial, 127
Caversham House, 34
Chipper, John, 155
Claisebrook, 36-39
Claremont, 52-55
Claremont Jetty, 53
Claremont Museum, 53, 55
Claremont Public Baths, 53

Cloisters Foreshore, 69
coastal eco-system, 104
Colonial Jail, 27
Concrete Poem, 38
Cottesloe Beach, 114-117
Cottesloe Reef Fish Habitation Area, 116
Cottesloe Sundial, 115
Crystal Cave, 81, 82
Currie, Capt Mark John, 44

D
Dale, Ensign Robert, 27, 155, 180
Darling Range, 135-187
Deep Water Point, 68-71
Derbal Yerrigan dreaming, 58
Djenark, 113
dugites, 34
Dwerda, 87

E
E Shed Markets, 23
Eastern Railway, 140-143
Echidna Trail, 136-139
Ellis Brook, 176-178
environment, care for, 4
Esplanade Reserve, 14

F
Farman, Nola, 39
Federation Walkway, 19
Fenians, 127
Finlayson, Robert, 38
Fire Fighters Memorial Grove, 19
Fisherman's Monument, 24
Fishing Boat Harbour, 24, 67
footware, 3
Forrest, Sir John, 140
Fremantle, 22-25, 64-67
Fremantle Markets, 24
Fremantle Oval, 25
Fremantle, Capt Sir Charles, 67
Freshwater Bay, 52, 56-59

G
Garden Island, 127
Geidens, Indra, 14
Gerovich, John, 25
Gibbs, May, 14
Golden Pipeline Trail, 156-159
Goldfields Water Supply Scheme, 154, 155, 156-159
Great Depression, 71

Index

Great Lakes District, 77
Guilderton, 102-105
Guilderton Lighthouse, 103
Guildford, 26-29
Hale, Bishop, 15

H
Heirisson Island, 40, 41
Henry Lawson Walk, 39
Henry, Lieutenant John, 70
Herdsman Lake, 88-91
Herdsman Lake Wildlife Centre, 88, 89
HMAS Ovens, 66
HMS Challenger, 67
Hovea Station, 142

I-J
Illa Kuri Track, 37
Indiana Tearooms, 115
Irish Fenians, 127
James, Greg, 23, 24
Jane Brook Bridge, 142
Jane Brook Valley, 140-143
Jinlan, 82
John Forrest Heritage Trail, 140-143
John Forrest National Park, 140-143
John Forrest National Park walking trails, 143
John George Walk Trail, 32-35
John Graham Reserve, 118, 119
Jones, Dicky, 137
Jones, Tony, 23

K
Kairp Ngun Gar cave, 61
Kalamunda National Park, 164-167
Kattamorda Heritage Trail, 173
Keates, William and James, 41
Kep Track, 153, 157-158
Kings Park, 15-16, 18-20
Kings Square, 23
koalas, 82
Kokoda Trail Memorial, 16
Kookaburras, 86

L
Lake Joondalup, 85
Lake Leschenaultia, 144-151
Lawson Building, 15
Lesmurdie Falls, 168-171
Lesmurdie National Park, 168-171
little penguins, 130

location maps, 189-193
Loch McNess, 78-79
London Court, 14
long-necked turtles, 138

M
Mardalup Park, 38
Maritime Museum, 24, 66
marri tree, 150
Mason & Bird Heritage Trail, 172-175
Mason & Bird Timber Company, 72, 172
Matilda Bay, 44-45
Matilda Bay, 44-45
McKenzie, Seaforth, 133
McNess, Sir Charles, 79
Milo Beach, 61
Mindarie Dunes, 106-109
Minim Cove, 60
Monument to the Old Jetty, 24
Moore River, 102, 105
Mount Dale, 180-183
Mount Eliza, 16
Mount Henry Bridge, 68
Mounts Bay Road, 15-16
Mrs Herbert's Dog Park, 53
Mundaring, 152-163
Mundaring history, 155
Mundaring Weir, 157
Mundaring Weir Rail Trail, 152-155
Munday Brook Bridge, 173

N-O
National Park Waterfalls, 141
Neil Hawkins Park, 85
Neil, Anne, 17
Nyoongar People, 16, 52, 61, 77, 80, 82, 84, 87, 96, 113, 136
Nyoongar tours, 96
O'Connor, C.Y., 23, 153, 156
O'Reilly, John, 127
Old Perth Boys School, 13
Old Tearoom Jetty, 57

P-Q
Palm Beach Jetty, 128
paperbark swamp, 96
Parliament House, 16
Paten's Brook Campsite, 161
Paten's Brook Track, 160-163
Pelican Point, 44
Penguin Experience Centre, 131
Penguin Island, 130-133

Index

P-Q

Peppermint Grove, 56-59
Peron, Francois, 122
Perth CBD, 12-17
Piesse Brook, 164-167
Piesse, William Roper, 164
Pietro Giacomo Porcelli, 23
pig face, 97-98
Point Peron, 122
Point Walter, 48-51
public transport, 1
Quandong plant, 120
Queen Victoria Memorial, 16
Queensgate Car Park, 25
Quindalup dune system, 106

R

Reg Bond Reserve, 34
River Ramble, 26
Rock Gardens, 142
Rockingham, 122-133
Rockingham Lakes Regional Park, 122
Rocky Bay, 60-63
Rocky Pool, 164-167
Roe Garden, 19
Rotary Park, 128
Roundhouse, 24, 66

S

Sandalford Winery, 34
Sanford, William, 13
Sculpture Park, Mundaring, 153
Shenton Jr, George, 44
Shipwreck Galleries, 24, 67
Sixty Foot Falls, 176-179
Smith, Charles, 14, 127
Snuggle Pot and Cuddle Pie, 14
South Fremantle Football Club, 25
Southern Crossings, 23
Spectacles, The, 96-99
Spremberg, Alex, 25
St Georges Terrace, 13-14
State War Memorial, 16
Stirling Gardens, 14
Stirling, Sir James, 14, 32, 51, 67, 75
sunscreen, 3
Swan Bell Tower, 41
Swan View Tunnel, 141
Syd's Rapids, 138
Synergy Parkland, 20

T

Thomsons Lake, 92-95
Town Walk, 26
track closures, 5
Trafalgar Road Culvert, 39
Transperth, 1
Trigg Bushland Reserve, 110-113
Trigg Mountain, 110-113
Trigg, Henry S., 14
Trinity Uniting Church, 14

U-V

Unknown Photographer, 17
Verguide Draeck, 105
Victoria Gardens, 37
Victoria Quay, 23-24
Village Art Market, 23
Vlamingh Memorial, 116
Vlamingh, Willem de, 40, 41, 51, 114, 150

W

Wagyls, 16, 58, 61
walking brochure, 20
walking grades, 2
walking with children, 2
Walsh-Smith, Joan, 14, 127
Walyunga National Park, 136-141
Wanneroo Song Line, 84
Wardarn dreaming, 113
water (drinking), 2
Waterfront Pioneer Rotary Public Art Work, 127
Waugal, 85
Whalers Tunnel, 66
Wheel of Perth, 41
White, Henry, 82
Wong Sue, Jack, 128
Woodbridge Riverside Park, 32
Woodloes Homestead and Museum, 73
Woodloes Walk, 72-75
Woodman Point, 118-121
Woodsome Hill, 138

Y-Z

Yagan, 41
Yanchep National Park, 78-83
yandip (bullrushes), 80
Yellagonga Regional Park, 85-86
Z Force, 128
Zamia nuts, 150
Yaruga Picnic Area, 50

Transperth Zone Map

CAT Routes

Important Information

Due to ongoing road works in the Perth CBD there may be disruptions to CAT services.

Transperth apologises for any inconvenience.

LEGEND

CENTRAL AREA TRANSIT

Effective date 2 May 2010

- Blue CAT Route
- Red CAT Route
- Yellow CAT Route
- 22 31 35 CAT Bus Stop
- 2 30 Red/Yellow CAT Bus Stop
- Railway
- Roads

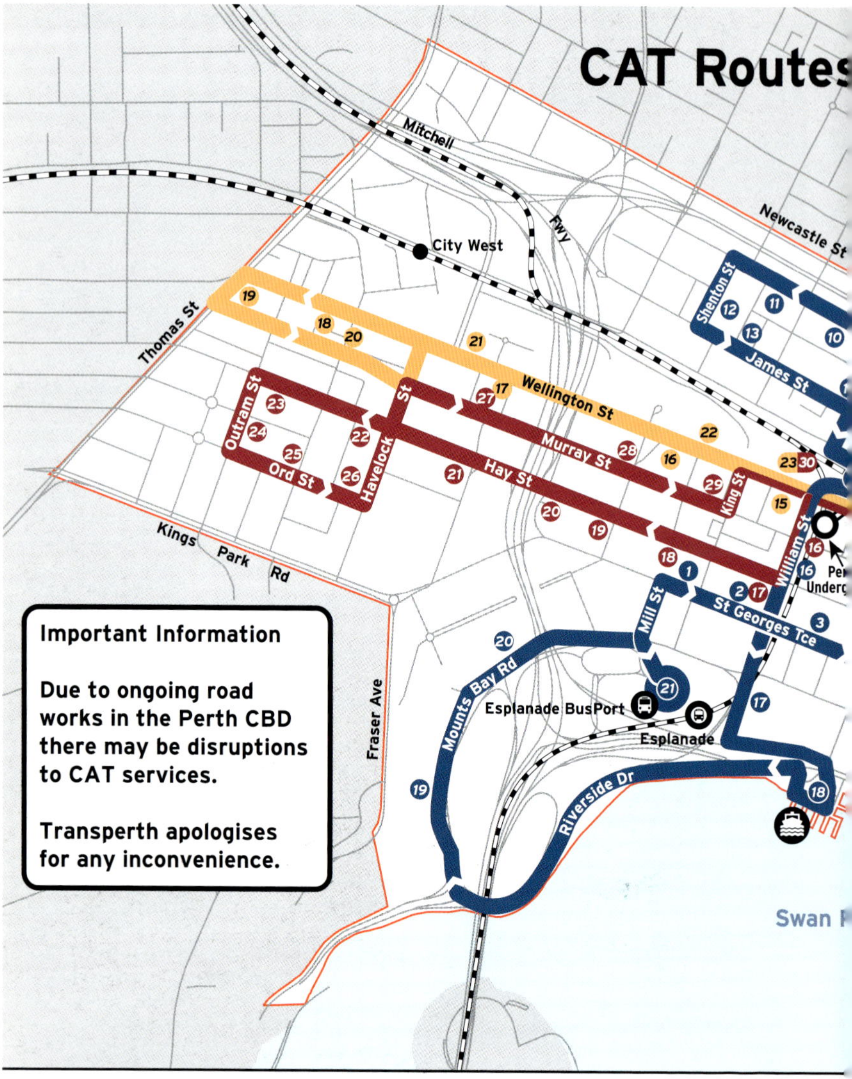

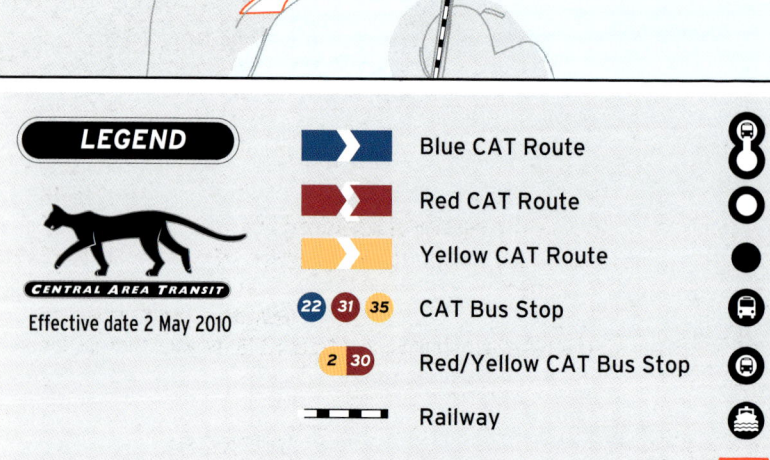

Want to know more about Transperth?

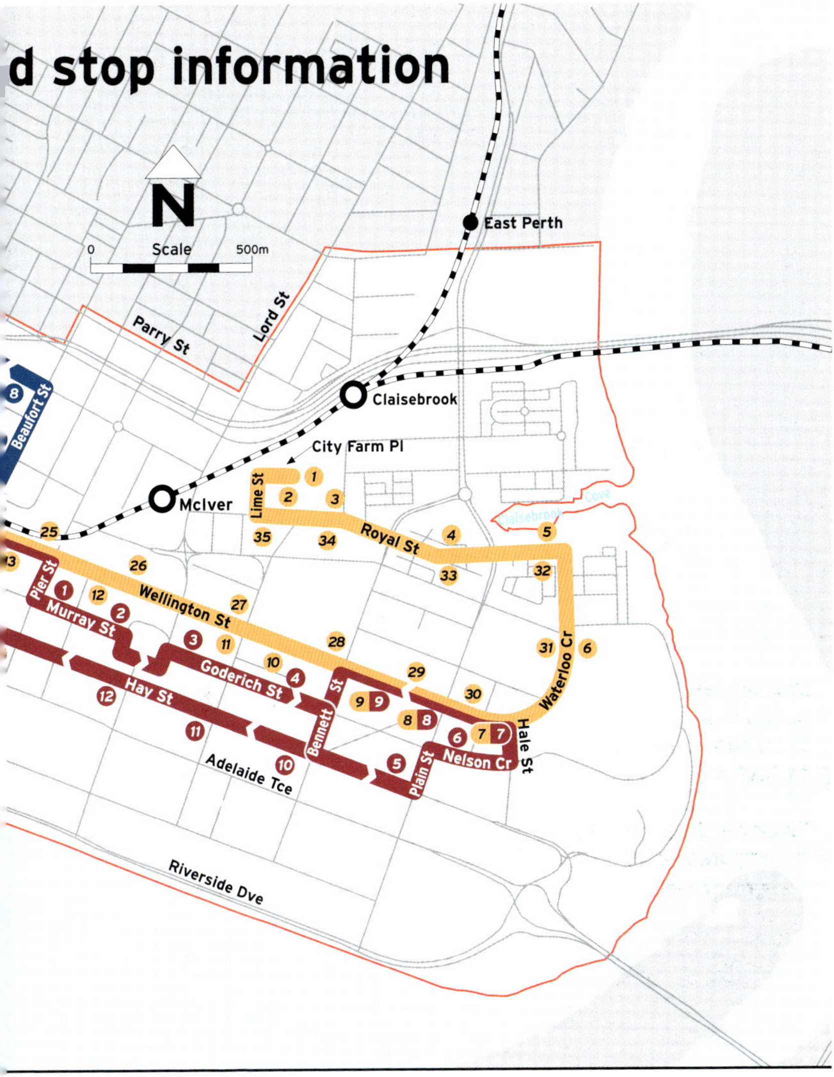

InfoLine	13 62 13
CommentLine	13 16 08
People with hearing disabilities TTY	9428 1999
Translating and Interpreting Service TIS	13 14 50
MobileWeb	136213.mobi
Website	www.transperth.wa.gov.au
SMS SMS your stop number to 13 62 13 for your next 5 trips	

About the author

The author would like to express his sorrow and shame for all that has been done to the Nyoongar over the years in the name of civilization by colonizing Europeans. The Nyoongar are the indigenous Australian people who live in the south-west corner of WA their country extends from Jurien Bay in the north to the southern coast, and east to Ravensthorpe and Southern Cross. 'Nyoongar' is also the name for their common language. Their name in the various original dialects is thought to mean "people".

Paul Amyes is a freelance photographer and writer who has lived in Western Australia since 1988. Paul cut his bushwalking teeth on following Roman roads in the United Kingdom at an early age and sees walking as the perfect way to explore the world, and journalism as the perfect excuse to be nosey. His overall wish is that people using this book will develop a love and understanding of the environment.

Acknowledgements

Thank you to all the staff at DEC who have given me assistance as I researched the book. I would like to thank Dr Leah Power for without her expert care this project would not have been possible. For Paul Sherlock, Brenda Fleming, Trevor Gee, Jan, Margaret, Maggie and Hans de Jong, Paul Connolly and Robert Fletcher for being there. Lastly I would like to thank my wife Helen for believing in me.

Photography and cartography in this book

All of the photographs in this book were taken by the author. All photographs are copyright © Paul Amyes and may not be reproduced without permission.

The Transperth and CAT maps in this book are reproduced with the kind permission of, and are copyright © Transperth, and may not be reproduced without permission.

All of the other maps in this book were created by Tony Fakira. They are copyright © Woodslane Press and may not be reproduced without permission.

Woodslane Press

This book is just one of a growing series of outdoor guides from Sydney publishers Woodslane. To browse through other titles available from Woodslane, visit www.woodslane.com.au. If your local bookshop does not have stock of a Woodslane book, they can easily order it for you. In case of difficulty please contact our customer service team on 02 9970 5111 or info@woodslane.com.au or order directly at www.travelandoutdoor.com.

Titles include:

Adelaide's Best Bush, Coast & City Walks
$29.95 • ISBN: 9781921683350

Canberra's Best Bush, Park & City Walks
$29.95 • ISBN: 9781921683381

Sydney's Best Harbour & Coastal Walks
$29.95 • ISBN: 9781921606274

Melbourne's Best Bush, Bay & City Walks
$29.95 • ISBN: 9781921874352

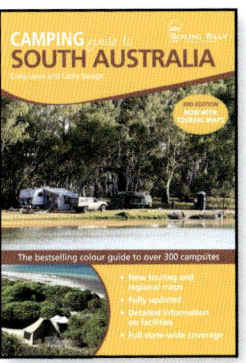

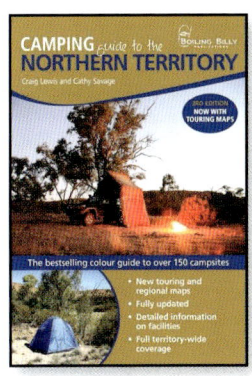

Camping Guide to Western Australia 2/e

$19.95

ISBN: 9781876296292

Camping Guide South Australia 3/e

$29.95

ISBN: 9781921203985

Camping Guide to the Northern Territory 3/e

$29.95

ISBN: 9781921203978

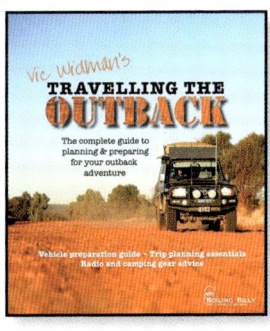

Travelling the Outback

$34.95

ISBN: 9781921606649

Australian Bush Cooking

$34.95

ISBN: 9781921203930

The 4WD Handbook

$44.95

ISBN: 9781921606175

Your thoughts appreciated!

We do hope that you are enjoying using this book, but we know that nothing in this world is perfect and your suggestions for improving on this edition would be much appreciated.

Your name _____

Your address or email address _____

_____

_____

Your contact phone number _____

Are you a resident or visitor to Perth? _____

What you most liked about this book _____

_____

_____

What you least liked about this book _____

_____

_____

Which is your favourite walk featured in this book?

_____

Which walk wasn't featured but you think should have been included?

_____

Would you like us to keep you informed of other Woodslane books?
If so: are you interested in:

- ☐ walking
- ☐ visiting natural & historic sites
- ☐ picnicking
- ☐ cycling
- ☐ general outdoor activities
- ☐ activities in Perth region only
- ☐ activities in WA
- ☐ activities around Australia

What others books would you like to see in this series?

_____

_____

Woodslane Pty Ltd • 7/5 Vuko Place • Warriewood • NSW 2102
Fax: 02 9970 5002 • Email: info@woodslane.com.au